Dear Moms at Prayer

*52 letters from an overseas mom and
grandma
on praying for Third Culture Kids*

DEANNA HARRISON

CONTENTS

Acknowledgements...v

Definitions and Abbreviations...vii

Foreword...ix

Introduction...1

Week 1: Consistency...3

Week 2: Creativity..5

Week 3: Compassion...7

Week 4: Boldness..9

Week 5: Self-control..11

Week 6: Courage...13

Week 7: Relational maturity 15

Week 8: Decisiveness 17

Week 9: Deference...19

Week 10: Discernment...21

Week 11: Diligence 23

Week 12: Discretion 26

Week 13: Endurance 28

Week 14: Forgiveness...30

Week 15: Enthusiasm...33

Week 16: Faith..35

Week 17: Protected..38

Week 18: Routine orderliness 39

Week 19: Generosity 41

Week 20: Initiative 43

Week 21: Wonder 45

Week 22: Farsightedness...47

Week 23: Tenacity..49

Week 24: Understanding...51

Week 25: Thoroughness 53

Week 26: Cautiousness..55

Week 27: Humility 57

Week 28: Virtue...59

Week 29: Justice 61

Week 30: Sensitivity..63

Week 31: Obedience..65

Week 32: Quiet..67

Week 33: Submission 69

Week 34: Gentleness 71

Week 35: Benevolence 73

Week 36: Emotional health...74

Week 37: Persuasiveness..76

Week 38: Spiritual precocity...78

Week 39: Tenderness...80

Week 40: Punctuality..82

Week 41: Responsibility..84

Week 42: Security..86

Week 43: Confidence 88

Week 44: Freedom...90

Week 45: Assurance...92

Week 46: Trustfulness...94

Week 47: Gratefulness 97

Week 48: Thankfulness 99

Week 49: Awareness...101

Week 50: Dependability...103

Week 51: Contentment 105

Week 52: Resourcefulness 107

ACKNOWLEDGMENTS

The list of character traits that initially inspired these devotionals was developed by the Institute of Basic Life Principles (https://iblp.org/). I later branched out and developed many of my own definitions. However, I am grateful to IBLP for their inspiration, their permission to use their definitions and their encouragement in my ministry.

A huge debt of gratitude goes to Kandy Radzinsky, a gifted artist and a good friend who created the artwork for the cover of this book. I am awed by her talent, her creativity and her willingness to give freely for a friend in need.

I am also thankful to my brother-in-law, Jerry Dorris, who leant his expertise to the design and layout of the cover. His professional touch turned my amateur attempts into a thing of beauty.

Thanks to my mom who gave me the list of character traits that sparked the whole idea. My parents' example of faithful prayer for their kids and grandkids helps me grow in my own prayer life.

I am grateful for all the moms who participated in the original Moms at Prayer group. Their encouragement and inspiration kept me going.

Many thanks to my long-suffering kids who gave me permission to write about our strange and wonderful international life. Loving my kids and my grand-kids is, without a doubt, one of the biggest blessings of my life.

And most importantly, I am grateful to my husband. Hey, without you, I wouldn't even have these kids. Praying together daily for our kids is one of my greatest privileges. Thanks for always being there for me, listening to all my crazy ideas, believing in me, challenging me, cheering me on and loving me unconditionally.

DEFINITIONS AND ABBREVIATIONS

Third Culture Kid (TCK): A person growing up with the influence of one or more cultures, especially children who spend a significant amount of time in a culture that is not the culture of their passport country.

International Workers: Those who chose to serve in a culture other than their own in order to share their faith cross-culturally.

Faculté de Théologie Evangélique de l'Alliance Chrétienne (FATEAC): The seminary where my husband and I teach in Abidjan, Cote d'Ivoire. The official name in English is West Africa Alliance Seminary, but we usually just say "FATEAC."

Yugu-yugu: Local open-air market where used clothes are sold.

KJV: King James Version

FOREWORD

I am an international kid—one of those third-culture kids (TCK) Deanna Harrison heralds as a praying mother and grandmother! I grew up in India, survived boarding school, and later, in the Philippines, squeezed two years of high school correspondence into three years. But what a privilege to discover amazing people, realize God's call on my life, and set a course that brought me to where I am today. As Deanna makes clear, praying for kids like me is crucial to our development, which is to say it doesn't stop there—we all need praying mothers at whatever age! Even now after we raised three boys in Papua New Guinea, with the youngest now raising his two kids (my grandchildren) in Thailand, we continue to value those who pray. We TCKs are a highly blessed breed. By far the largest single group of people included in Who's Who is kids of international ministry workers. Three cheers for us, but it only happens because there are praying moms, in the home, mothers and grandmothers, like you, praying over newsletters, or via Skype or WhatsApp as the context accommodates. Prayers are sent to the Throne of Grace on behalf of us who, though we did not ask to be TCKs, can thrive and beblessed while blessing others. In contrast, as too often happens,parents focus on doing God's work and their children miss theopportunities and feel deprived. I have seen both, and soappreciate the power of prayer to make a difference.

What my former student and good friend Deanna Harrison has done in this devotional book, is demonstrate the value of prayer by telling stories that clearly communicate how God protects, enhances, and encourages TCKs because of praying moms like Deanna and those whom she brings into the conversation—YOU!! Her encouraging words penetrate the hearts of moms and dads as they bring their kids and those of their friends around the world before the Lord.

I love the way Deanna starts each chapter with a verse that characterizes the relevance of what follows. And the vignettes—often personal disclosures that let Deanna's humanity show through as well as her deep care and concern for her children and their children. These go beyond "overseas worker stories", often shared on furlough or in a newsletter "kid's corner". They reflect a deep relationship with God while allowing humanity to prevail. Deanna communicates that it is not the international worker or their task that is critical when raising TCKs, rather it isthe parent's relationship with God that gets passed on to the kids.They too are part of the overseas ministry enterprise, not add-onsin an "international ministry" environment. They represent thelove of parents for each other, for their Lord and for the peoplewhere God enables them to minister. In short, TCKs are the resultof parents serving God in a dynamic and vital way and passing thatpassion on to their children. More TCKs become international workers than any other source of overseas recruitment. This doesnot happen by accident, it comes from the prayers of the saints, ofmoms dedicated to praying for God to build Christian characterinto the kids. And that character trait finds its way into Deanna'ssalutations— 'characteristically yours'.

So, I encourage you to study the Scripture passages from which Deanna draws these characteristics. Allow her stories to trigger your own reflections, and make her prayers your own so you too can be a Mom of Prayer—for your own children (blessed to call you "Mom") and for those TCKs who need special protection and care as they navigate the duality (or more) of our contemporary, global world, while surviving the villages, townships, and urban streets where their parents minister. May your prayers honor our Lord and bless a TCK today!

Dan Shaw
Sr. Prof. Anthropology & Translation
Fuller Graduate School of Intercultural Studies
Pasadena, Sept. 2019

INTRODUCTION
The story behind this book

For over 40 years, my husband and I have served the Lord overseas: in Congo, France, Burkina Faso and Cote d'Ivoire. Our children were born in Africa, grew up internationally and are all serving cross-culturally. Our grand-children are growing up in cross-cultural contexts. I have been a pastor's wife, a teacher, a homeschooler, an educational consultant and an international worker. Yet, one of my biggest roles and greatest joys is being mom and grandma to a bunch of culturally-confused offsprings.

All kids need prayer. Nevertheless, kids who have grown up internationally, straddling two or three different cultures, not really African, not quite European, yet not exactly normal Americans, what we now sometimes call Third Culture Kids— these kids most decidedly need prayer.

Therefore, ten years ago, when I was asked to coordinate prayer requests among the moms serving in Africa, I was thrilled. Each week, moms sent in prayer requests. I compiled them, sent them out and every Wednesday we prayed for our kids.

Around the same time, my mom gave me a list of positive character traits. That list sparked the idea of writing a short devotional on praying for the character of our kids as an introduction to the weekly list of prayer requests.

Over the years, several moms have encouraged me to compile my devotionals into a book. So, I picked out some of my favorite letters, and threw out some that I knew my kids would *not* want in a published book. The stories in these letters were chosen to illustrate ways to pray for the character of our children. They draw from events over a span of 35 years and are in no particular chronological order. Therefore, don't be surprised if you read a story about our daughter getting married followed by a story of our son in kindergarten. I should mention that some of the names have been changed for security reasons.

Even though our family's experience is limited to Africa, Europe and the Middle East, I believe that the vast majority of these principles would hold true in any cultural setting. In fact, my desire is that this book will inspire prayer for our kids, whatever their roots or their stories. This grandma is convinced of the power of prayer!

WEEK 1—JANUARY 1-7

Consistency (vs. Instability): following constantly the same
principles in all circumstances

*"Do not be anxious about anything, but in everything by prayer and
supplication with thanksgiving let your requests be made known to
God. And the peace of God, which surpasses all understanding, will
guard your hearts and your minds in Christ Jesus."*
Philippians 4:6-7

Dear Moms at Prayer,

We are going through flooding in Burkina Faso. Isn't it
surprising how these dry, parched, Sahelian countries that
desperately need rain most of the year would all of a sudden have
too much rain? I don't actually think they have too much rain, the
rain is just not controlled and channeled and harnessed as it could
be for the greater good of everyone.

This is, to me, an image of our prayer life. Sometimes it
can get dry out there, can't it? We get busy with the daily grind of
meeting our children's physical needs and find it hard to discipline
ourselves to consistently lift them up in prayer. At other times,
often because of challenging circumstances, we can literally flood
the gates of heaven with our ardent prayers. Concentrated prayer

is a wonderful thing, and I'm all for it. However, when it comes to our children, a steady stream of daily prayer is better than a once a month downpour. This week let's ask the Lord to help us set the example of daily prayer, so that our children will learn the necessity of a consistent walk with the Lord.

Still learning,

Deanna

WEEK 2—JANUARY 8-14

Creativity (vs. Underachievement): approaching a need, a task,
or an idea from a new perspective[*]

"In the beginning God created the heavens and the earth."
Genesis 1:1

Dear Moms at Prayer,

When I was a young mom raising kids in the Congo, I was, to
some degree, addicted to parenting how-to books. I think I read
everything James Dobson ever wrote, and he was just one of the
many authors who influenced my life. However, I always read
those books with a certain bittersweet frustration because I could
never actually follow their advice to the letter. I remember sitting
in the middle of the African jungle (or at least it felt that way)
reading some Dobsonian guidance for young moms that went
something like this: "Mothers should be sure and have some time
for themselves to develop interests and hobbies apart from their
husbands and children. Join an exercise class or a homeschool
support group or take a class in painting or needlework." I just sat
there and thought, "Yeah, right!" The only other ladies I knew

---

[*] All definitions marked with an asterisk are used with permission
from the Institute in Basic Life Principles.

were hard-working Congolese whose "exercise classes" consisted of chopping wood and carrying water on their heads. Most of my girlfriends couldn't read, let alone homeschool their kids. And if there were going to be any needlework classes, I was pretty sure I would be teaching them!

However, I look back on those times with wonder at the faithfulness of God. Our kids had amazing childhoods, and all of them say they wouldn't trade it for anything. We didn't have the same resources (on many different levels) that we would have had in the States, but the Lord always seemed to provide some surprisingly creative alternatives.

Of course, the task of raising our kids internationally is ever changing. The challenges of today are not the ones I faced in the jungle thirty years ago. That's why we must continue to pray for creativity. God is doing a new thing in our midst and we want to be on board with all He is doing in our ministries, in our families and in the lives of our kids. Let that be our prayer this week, for us and for our children.

Our God is a creative God. He created the world from nothing, and I would say that qualifies as genuine "out of the box" thinking. He is the one who can inspire us to "approach a need, a task, or an idea from a new perspective."

Creatively yours,

Deanna

WEEK 3—JANUARY 15-21

Compassion (vs. Indifference): helping those who are hurting

"Therefore, as God's chosen people, holy and dearly loved, clothe yourselves with compassion, kindness, humility, gentleness and patience."
Colossians 3:12

Dear Moms at Prayer,

My husband and I were in the store here in Abidjan yesterday. We were just about to get in line when a handicapped boy, maybe 12 or 14 years old, came around the aisle. He looked like he had cerebral palsy. Somehow, he slipped and fell flat on his face. For a split second he lay sprawled on the tile with his crutches flung on either side. Then someone picked him up and I picked up his crutches. Although he must have suffered, both from the physical pain and the humiliation of the fall, he said not a word. He gave us all a big smile, and then hobbled back down the aisle. We got in line, paid for our groceries and drove home.

I couldn't shake the image of that poor kid lying helpless on the floor. I went over and over it in my mind. What more could I have done? I picked up his crutches—big deal. When I got home, I prayed for him. I also prayed for myself. I prayed against the indifference that creeps into your soul when you are daily surrounded by suffering. I prayed that God would break my heart again and fill me anew with His compassion.

I pray also for our children. Personally, I have been thankful for the people God has brought into our children's lives to teach them about compassion. Our daughter, Becky, had the privilege of working at two different orphanages during her high school years, one in a couple of week-long stints and one in a weekly commitment during her senior year. The youth group organized incredible projects where the kids raised money for food which they then distributed to the poor. These were life changing experiences for the youth group. I know Becky will never be the same. Now her life goal is to help improve orphanages around the world.

This week let's pray that we all, parents and kids alike, have a fresh outpouring of godly compassion. May we be like Jesus who, seeing the suffering, was moved with compassion.

Compassionately yours,

Deanna

WEEK 4—JANUARY 22-28

Boldness (vs. Fearfulness): willingness to take risks and act innovatively; confidence or courage

"On the day I called, You answered me; You made me bold with strength in my soul."
Psalm 138:3

Dear Moms at Prayer,

We did a crazy thing when our children were young, and we are still feeling the repercussions. We read together as a family the book *God's Smuggler* by Brother Andrew and the book *Bruchko* by Bruce Olson. If you've read them (and everyone should read them!), you'll know that they are the stories of godly, bold, courageous—and I guess you could even say reckless—men who went to dangerous places and did marvelous things for God. My husband and I have the impression that those two books changed our son's life forever. Now our son and daughter-in-law serve in a very dangerous creative access country. You know the line, "I could tell you, but I'd have to kill you afterwards"? That's what I have to say when people ask me where my children live. Because of the dangers, I'm embarrassed to admit that my prayers for my children are often a strange mixture of godly boldness and lurking fearfulness.

Let's face it. When you raise a family overseas, there's a lot to be afraid of—weird diseases, unstable governments, "child safety," terrifying traffic and violent crime. And those are just the surface issues! One verse that has helped me a lot with this is I John 4:18, *"There is no fear in love. But perfect love drives out fear..."*

As we pray for our children this week, let's pray for a boldness born out of perfect love. We love God. God loves us. God loves our children. God has called us overseas. With that knowledge, we can pray boldly for our children, we can model bold faith to our children, and we can lay our fears concerning our children at the feet of Jesus.

Boldly yours,

Deanna

WEEK 5--JANUARY 29-FEBRUARY 4

Self-control (vs. Self-indulgence): having power and control over one's own actions by moderating one's impulses, emotions, or desires

"Like a city whose walls are broken down is a man who lacks self-control."
Proverbs 25:28

Dear Moms at Prayer,

Part of me just doesn't want to treat the next character trait on the list—self-control. Every example of dealing with self-control in myself or in my kids was quite embarrassing, either for them or for me. Consequently, we are just not going to go there.

While thinking about this subject, it did occur to me that there are two types of self-control. One type is disciplining yourself and your outer actions. Another name for this type of self-control is self-discipline. The other type of self-control is controlling the inner desires of our heart, mind and soul. Anyone who follows the lives of athletes knows that there is a difference. These are some of the most disciplined creatures on earth, working long hours, denying themselves, following rules in everything from schedules to diet to exercise routines. Then every once in a while, we hear about some super athlete exercising an incredible lack of self-control. These athletes are self-disciplined in some areas of their lives, but, because of the state of their inner life, they demonstrate lack of self-control. John McEnroe, O.J. Simpson and Mike Tyson (ear sandwich, anyone?) are famous examples that come to mind, but we all know of many others.

The Bible says that self-control is a fruit of the Spirit. I genuinely believe that even if we achieve self-discipline on our own, we need the Holy Spirit to walk in true self-control of our inner self. We might have the discipline to control our outer actions, but the kind of godly self-control that changes our inner attitudes and perceptions is born of the Spirit.

For that reason, prayer for our children is essential. We can help them to live in discipline, but we also need to pray that the Holy Spirit will be birthing the fruit of the Spirit in their lives. We can prune and nurture and fertilize our little fruit bearers, but ultimately, the great Fruit Giver must be at work in their lives.

This week let's pray for self-control in our children's lives. And while I'm at it, I'm going to pray for more self-control in my own life. Want to join me?

Praying for fruit,

Deanna

WEEK 6—FEBRUARY 5-11

Courage (vs. Fear): mental or moral resilience to face opposition, danger or difficulties, despite one's own fear

"Have I not commanded you? Be strong and courageous. Do not be afraid; do not be discouraged, for the Lord your God will be with you wherever you go."
Joshua 1:9

Dear Moms at Prayer,

Randy and I have been reading through Joshua together (and, BTW, it can be very gruesome reading if you think about it). One theme that comes through continually is courage. God and Joshua keep coming back to: Be strong and courageous, and then, to emphasize, they approach from the other direction with: Do not be afraid.

Right now, it seems like there are a lot of things to fear. Logically, if I watch American news, I am afraid for the future of our country. Logically, if I read up on African news, I am afraid of terrorists and instability and war. Logically, if I look at the lives of international workers, I am afraid of persecution and martyrdom and untold sacrifices. Logically, if I think about turning 62 next week, I'm afraid of growing old... And yet God calls His people to walk in strength and courage.

This week I propose that we pray for courage for our children. It can be little things like witnessing to friends at school or facing the challenges of yet another new neighborhood or the exciting, but unknown world of college or facing the big wide world after graduation.

While writing about this subject, I thought of I John 4:18, *"There is no fear in love. But perfect love drives out fear, because fear has to do with punishment. The one who fears is not made perfect in love."*

Dear friends, be of good courage this week. Walk in perfect love and pray that our children will learn to walk in perfect love, which casts out fear.

Courageously yours,

Deanna

WEEK 7—FEBRUARY 12-18

Relational maturity (vs. Relational immaturity): the ability to form realistic expectations of others, based on an honest and Spirit-led assessment of their character and personality and a discernment of the appropriate level of commitment and involvement in a relationship

"There are three things that are too amazing for me,
four that I do not understand:
the way of an eagle in the sky,
the way of a snake on a rock,
the way of a ship on the high seas,
and the way of a man with a young woman."
Proverbs 30:18-19

Dear Moms at Prayer,

Valentine's Day is coming up. I thought that fact is a good reminder to pray for our kids and their love lives.

1.   For our kids who are already married, let's pray that the Lord will bless their relationship with their spouse, bringing them closer to the Lord and each other.

2.   For our kids who are not married, pray that the Lord will

guide them in this whole area of their lives.

3.   For those who are called to celibacy, pray that they will live in peace and contentment with their calling.

4.   For those who are called to marriage, pray that they will be led to the right spouse.

5.   For those who are in that challenging, turbulent "I'm too young to get married, but my hormones are raging" stage, ask that the Lord will help them to walk in purity and spiritual maturity.

6.   And remember, it is never too young to start praying for this area of our kid's lives. We started praying for our kids' spouses when they were babies. It has been remarkable to see how all of them have spouses who were just right for their callings, their personalities and their temperaments.

7.   Let's have special prayer time for our kids who are not thriving in their marriages. Some of our kids are struggling. Some are going through divorces. Even during these challenging times, God can meet our children in their need and redeem their situations in miraculous ways. When we can do nothing else, we can pray.

Thankful for His everlasting love,

Deanna

WEEK 8—FEBRUARY 19-25

Decisiveness (vs. Procrastination): the ability to recognize key factors and finalize difficult decisions*

"Whoever watches the wind will not plant; whoever looks at the clouds will not reap."
Ecclesiastes 11:4

Dear Moms at Prayer,

Sandwiched in between our 12 years in the Democratic Republic of Congo and our twelve years in West Africa, we ministered in France for ten years. Through a series of providential circumstances, we were able to get the French equivalent of green cards. Our kids were in French school, 75% of our salary was paid by our French church, and we were in the French medical and social security system. We stopped short of becoming French citizens, because that would have meant giving up our American citizenship.

Towards the end of our time in France, America changed their policy and allowed citizens to remain American and hold double citizenship. We heard about the policy change towards the end of the long process of becoming French residents. We had already filled out myriads of official forms (in triplicate), fought Paris traffic more times than I care to remember to meet with

17

immigration officials, had the home inspection and passed the required medical exams. As French residents, we had all the benefits the French socialized government had to offer. We just didn't have the French passport.

My husband and I kicked around the idea of applying for French citizenship, but the thought of starting over on more paper work, more interviews, more trips to the immigration office, more hassle made us hesitate. We said to ourselves that we could always apply later when we had more time. In the meantime, the Lord's gentle voice was calling us back to Africa. We were hired to teach at the Faculté de Théologie Evangélique de l'Alliance Chrétienne (FATEAC) in Cote d'Ivoire and the rest is history.

Fast forward to the present: Our kids are grown up. Our two oldest are both married and called to serve in some of the most dangerous countries in the world. I can't help regretting that we weren't more decisive about pursuing French citizenship for our kids. With today's political climate, it would be handy to be able to pull out a French passport instead of an American passport in certain countries. Alas, the opportunity has come and gone.

To make me feel better, my husband says we probably wouldn't have been able to get them in the time we had left in France. And, of course, God's grace is sufficient. He can protect our children, no matter what color passport they carry. Nevertheless, this experience has shown me the importance of being decisive at the appropriate time.

An Indian evangelist, Brother Bakht Singh once said, "As believers it is our greatest privilege to know God's will and to do it." Let that thought inspire our prayers for our children this week. May they know the will of God in their daily lives and do it--- decisively.

Non-hesitantly yours,

Deanna

WEEK 9—FEBRUARY 26-MARCH 4

Deference (vs. Rudeness): limiting my freedom so I do not
offend the tastes of those around me*

*"I have become all things to all people so that by all possible means I
might save some."*
I Corinthians 9:22b

Dear Moms at Prayer,

Learning to be polite is a complicated lesson for a Third-
Culture Kid.

1. For one thing, the rules change all the time. In West Africa,
it is perfectly acceptable to eat with your hands, but don't let your
mom catch you doing that at a church potluck on tour in the
States! Peeing behind a tree may be okay when playing with your
African friends, but Grandma just might not appreciate it when
the "tree" is her rosebush.

2. You are often on display. When you are in the States, you
are the darling TCK wearing cute African clothes and reciting
John 3:16 in Lingala for admiring little old ladies. When you are
in Africa, you can be fascinating for the nationals, especially in a
village that hasn't seen many foreigners. We used to say that we
felt like we had gone to the freak show and we were the freaks.

3. Sometimes you can get away with murder. Your nanny tries

to avoid upsetting the boss's kids. Aunties and uncles on the field don't want to correct someone else's children. Moms and Dads find it hard to be strict when their offsprings come home from boarding school. If you are a smart TCK (and most of them are!), you can totally work most situations for your own benefit.

And yet, as Christ's ambassadors, our children must learn deference. They must be flexible enough to use the appropriate politeness that fits with the right context. They must learn to be genuinely grateful for the kindness of their elders (even when they pinch your cheeks and display that dorky-looking prayer card taken when you were three years old). They must learn the joy of writing thank you notes, and trying new foods without making faces, and clearing off the table without being told. Even little ones can say "please" and "thank you" and ask to be excused from the table. Our children must demonstrate authentic respect for our national brothers and sisters. They must learn to avoid even the suggestion of snootiness, rudeness, condescension or superiority, on either side of the ocean.

Our prayers are for ourselves and our children. May the Lord give us wisdom as we teach and model deference and may the Lord give our children tender hearts that are willing to give up certain freedoms for the sake of those around them. May we all learn to avoid rudeness and demonstrate deference, so that Christ will be glorified in our lives.

Politely yours,

Deanna

WEEK 10—MARCH 5-11

Discernment (vs. Shortsightedness): understanding the deeper
reasons why things happen*

*"Do not worry about anything, but in everything by prayer and
supplication with thanksgiving let your requests be made known to
God. And the peace of God, which surpasses all understanding, will
guard your hearts and your minds in Christ Jesus."*
Philippians 4:6

Dear Moms at Prayer,

When I was a young wife in Congo, I had a miscarriage. I was
so naïve, and so isolated, I didn't even know I was pregnant. I only
knew that I kept bleeding and bleeding and kept getting sicker and
sicker. I eventually had to be flown 500 km to a hospital.

Once at the hospital, they did a D&C and that was the end of
that. I stayed in a guest house and waited for an available flight to
take me home. I had plenty of time to ponder this whole surprising
situation. I had been with child and then had lost the child. Why?

When I finally arrived home, I was amazed. All my African
neighbors had heard of my troubles and were there to welcome me
home. Their kindness was overwhelming. As the days and weeks
went by, I noticed a difference in my ministry. Before, I had found

it hard to relate to the African ladies. They were friendly, but our lives were so different. However, after the miscarriage, we had something in common. They had all lost children. They could understand and relate to my pain. And I was better able to comprehend, at least in some small measure, a little of the sorrows they carried. It was less of "them" and "me", and more of "us". Suddenly, I was "in." I began to realize that God had used a very bewildering and difficult experience for good in my life. In retrospect, God gave me the discernment and understanding to see why He had allowed this challenging time in my life.

This week I invite us to pray for discernment for ourselves and for our children. May He give us an understanding of the bigger picture of what He is doing in our lives and in the lives of our children. May He give us an eternal perspective, which reaches beyond our naturally limited and shortsighted view of situations. May we echo the prayer of Solomon, *"Give your servant a discerning heart."*

Discerningly yours,

Deanna

WEEK 11—MARCH 12-18

Diligence (vs. Slothfulness): investing my time and energy to complete each task assigned to me*

"And let us not grow weary of doing good, for in due season we will reap, if we do not give up."
Galatians 6:9

Dear Moms at Prayer,

For our second home assignment from the Congo, we decided to go to Kentucky so that my husband could study at Asbury Theological Seminary. We would be arriving in Kentucky with two little ones. I knew we'd need to find a church home in this new-to-us region. I had a long list of "musts" for this dream church I was going to attend during home assignment.

Required list for home assignment church:

• MUST have a nice, finished church building! (We had been involved in several huge projects, including building a Bible institute and a house. I wanted to settle down to comfort on Sunday morning.)

• MUST have a great children's program! (We never felt led to have a nanny for our children. In Africa, I not only took care of our kids—along with a handful of our son's African playmates, I taught our son pre-school, taught Sunday School, and taught a class at the Bible institute on how to teach Sunday School. I was ready for someone else to do something phenomenal with my kids.)

- MUST have a great music program! (Although I enjoy African worship style, I was excited about soaking in some awesome worship times in my mother tongue accompanied by a tasteful but dynamic worship team.)
- MUST have great preaching and teaching! (After four years of giving out, I was ready to receive.)

You can probably guess what happened. After church shopping around for our perfect, dream church, the Lord led us to a small congregation meeting in the rented auditorium of the local Catholic high school. Every Sunday we had to set up the folding chairs and the sound system and the little electric piano and the portable pulpit. They were just starting to organize a children's program when we joined, and we were immediately recruited to teach 4th and 5th grade boys. We were also asked to teach an adult class on international ministry on Sunday evenings. The second Sunday we were there the pianist didn't show up and I filled in. After that, I was put on the regular music roster for Sunday morning. The preaching was okay—but certainly not the mega-church quality inspiration that I had dreamed about.

We ended up taking a two-year home assignment so that Randy could finish his masters. During those two years, we worked hard in our new church home. We got involved in a variety of ways, including helping to organize their first international ministry conference.

That was twenty-four years ago. The church has grown and now has a beautiful building. We have many friends and happy memories associated with that fellowship. They give monthly both to us and to our children who work overseas. I take away from that church a hard-earned reminder that, at least for me, diligently working together with brothers and sisters towards common goals is much more satisfying than joining a multitude of pew-warming spectators.

Let's pray for diligence and against slothfulness in our children's lives. Pray that they will learn the satisfaction of a job well done, as they do it as unto the Lord.

Diligently yours,

Deanna

WEEK 12—MARCH 19-25

Discretion (vs. simplemindedness): recognizing and avoiding words, actions and attitudes that bring undesirable consequences*

"The one who has knowledge uses words with restraint, and whoever has understanding is even-tempered."
Proverbs 17:27

Dear Moms at Prayer,

My husband and I worked in France for ten years. While our confident, outgoing younger daughter, Becky, thrived in the competitive environment of French public schools, her shy, older sister, Cathy, found the social atmosphere challenging, especially in middle school. One morning Cathy was sharing about how difficult it was to feel accepted and to make friends.

Her younger sister immediately piped up, "Seriously? I don't find it hard at all. I have lots of friends and everybody likes me."

Cathy rolled her eyes and said disgustedly, "Yes, and you are very humble, too."

Seven-year-old Becky knitted her brow questioningly and then shot back at her sister, "I am NOT humble!"

Sometimes telling the truth without discretion is not the best option. As was the case when Becky bragged in front of her lonely sister, some things—even true things—are just better left unsaid. Compassionate silence would have been a better option. Similarly, there are some things that, not wrong in and of themselves, are best avoided in certain situations. Our children (and their parents) need to grow in discernment and learn to use wise discretion, to avoid hurting others or unwittingly giving offense.

Proverbs 1:4 says that one of the goals of the proverbs is *"for giving prudence to the simple, knowledge and discretion to the young."* Let that be our prayer for ourselves and our children.

Discretely yours,

Deanna

WEEK 13—MARCH 26-APRIL 1

Endurance (vs. Discouragement): the inward strength to
withstand stress and do my best*

*"Consider him who endured such opposition from sinners, so that
you will not grow weary and lose heart."*
Hebrews 13:3

Dear Moms at Prayer,

Do you know about Google news update? You can sign up to
have Google send you an email showing the headline news for any
place or topic that you designate. I regularly get these news updates
for Cote d'Ivoire and for the Middle Eastern country where my
children serve, which I'll call X.

To me, following the news is like picking a scab. You know it
is going to hurt and bleed, but you just can't resist messing with it.
Why do I go ahead and click on those stupid website addresses
when I can tell just from the title that it is going to be depressing?
Here are some headlines that have come in the last few days:

"UN refugee agency mounts response to crisis in Cote
d'Ivoire"

"UN envoy urges protection from sexual violence amid CI
crisis"

"Protests turn violent in X"

"Spreading protests flag discontent across the Arab world"

"Gunmen kill 5 in X robbery, al Qaeda blamed"

In the movies, there is usually a "conflict" and then a "resolution"—and they fit it all into a two-hour film with time out to make some popcorn. In real life, these things just drag out. Discouragement too easily erodes away our endurance.

And nothing calls for more endurance than praying for our kids. Learning disabilities, spiritual crisis, lingering health problems, eating disorders, negative self-concepts, temper tantrums, loneliness, unemployment, bad marriages—it seems like every parent has a burden for their children that calls for endurance in prayer.

My dear sisters, may each of us receive a fresh renewal of joy and peace in the Lord as we pray for one another. May we be protected from discouragement and be strengthened in our audacity and faith, as we endure in prayer for our children. Bon courage!

Enduringly yours,

Deanna

WEEK 14—APRIL 2-8

Forgiveness (vs. Rejection): clearing the record of those who
have wronged me and not holding a grudge

*"Get rid of all bitterness, rage and anger, brawling and slander,
along with every form of malice. Be kind and compassionate to one
another, forgiving each other, just as in Christ God forgave you."*
Ephesians 4:31-32

Dear Moms at Prayer,

One of the plants I became acquainted with during our ten
years in France is "ortie," a fascinating European version of
stinging nettles. This stuff grows everywhere, in any kind of soil
and just about any temperature. If you touch it, it burns like fire,
and it leaves a rash that keeps hurting for quite a while. It is NOT
my favorite plant.

We were involved in a Christian scouting group called
Flambeaux while in France. We did a lot of camping in the wild.
On one of these camping trips our daughter needed to go out
behind a bush, if you catch my drift. She decided to pick some
leaves to use as toilet paper but didn't realize she was picking
"ortie" leaves. Wiping one's bottom with "ortie" leaves is a
powerful, painful lesson in outdoor survival, and an embarrassing

memory for our poor daughter. For that reason, the name of the particular daughter will remain a mystery to our group of praying moms.

In our last church in France, the property was overrun with "ortie." We weeded, we chopped, we pulled (with gloves on!), we mowed—but we still had plenty of "ortie." One of the things I discovered the hard way is that "ortie" has an interesting root system. The roots go down from the plant. Then they shoot off horizontally in different directions. If that root is stressed in any way, it will push up a new plant from the horizontal shoots of the root. What this means practically is that if you chop or hoe or break off the "ortie," but leave some of the root underground, it is as if you have planted more "ortie." It grows in even thicker.

Consequently, you basically have two options. The first one is to get out all the root system. This is easier said than done, because they tend to get tangled up with the roots of other "ortie," and they break off quite easily as you pull them up.

The second option is to get a special "ortie" killer chemical, and just zap those babies until they die off. This is not particularly organic or eco-friendly, but desperate times call for desperate measures.

While we were waging war against the "ortie" in our church yard, I happened to be reading in Hebrews, and came upon Hebrews 12:15, "*See to it that no one comes short of the grace of God; that no root of bitterness, springing up, causes trouble, and by it many be defiled.*" Of course, I knew that verse already, but my battle with the "ortie" gave it a whole new meaning. There are some things in our lives that can't just be chopped or plucked or pulled. If you do, they will just spring up even more abundantly in some other area of our lives. For a root of bitterness, you need to kill the roots if you want to get rid of the stinging painful plant.

One of the most powerful tools for killing the root of bitterness is forgiveness. We must model forgiveness before our children and pray that our children will learn to forgive as they are forgiven. This week let's pray against all those pesky "ortie" taking root in our lives and the lives of our children and let forgiveness soak down to free us from the bondage of bitterness.

Forgivingly yours,

Deanna

WEEK 15—APRIL 9-15

Enthusiasm (vs. Apathy): expressing joy in each task as I give it my best effort*

"Never be lacking in zeal, but keep your spiritual fervor, serving the Lord."
Romans 12:11

Dear Moms at Prayer,

We lived in Burkina Faso when our youngest daughter was in high school. Becky and two of her friends spent their spring break helping at an orphanage in a village not too far from Ouagadougou, the capital city. Anybody who has lived in Burkina knows that "spring" is the height of hot season. Temperatures hit the three digits regularly and sometimes reach 110 or higher. The girls ate millet porridge with the kids, helped with the babies and hung out with the teenagers. It must have been miserable in some ways. If I remember correctly, half way through the week a couple of the parents offered to take the girls back to Ouagadougou so that they could have some fun during the remainder of their spring break, but the girls didn't want to leave. They were having a great time.

Later the whole youth group went to that same orphanage

several times to help out for long week-ends. My husband and I were sponsors for one of those week-ends and I can tell you that the kids (TCKs and orphans alike) thoroughly enjoyed themselves. Those orphanage trips are some of our daughter's happiest high school memories. In fact, she hopes to return to Africa and work in orphanage-related ministries after college.

I'm sure you've seen the same phenomena in your country with your TCKs. There's something very fulfilling and joy-producing when you jump in and give yourself enthusiastically to a task. We want that kind of joy to be an integral part of our children's lives.

It is so sad to see a bunch of young people sitting around trying to look cool, but are actually just bored, apathetic, lacking direction and waiting to be entertained. It reminds me of that old joke, "Who cares about apathy?" We must pray for something higher, fuller, and more meaningful for our children.

This week may you enthusiastically approach the Lord in prayerful expectation of all He is going to do in the lives of our children.

Enthusiastically yours,

Deanna

WEEK 16—APRIL 16-22

Faith (vs. Presumption): confidence that God exists and that following His will yield the best outcome, even when I cannot see how

"Faith comes by hearing and hearing by the word of God."
Romans 10:17.

Dear Moms at Prayer,

Our family lived and worked in France for ten years. French public schools and the general attitude of the culture did little to build our children's faith. Even as an international worker, I found myself questioning and pondering foundational truths, and I didn't want that for my children. It was during that time that Romans 10:17 jumped out at me. I don't know all the contextual and theological implications of this verse, but for me it spoke of the importance of hearing (and reading) the Word of God as a means of building faith. I found this to be true in my own life. The more I listen to and read and study the Word of God, the less I struggle with the doubts, the "whys" and the philosophical questions of life and the more I have a simple confidence in the goodness of God.

Since this week's topic is faith, I thought I'd share just a few ideas from how our family made sure that hearing the Word of God was a part of our family life.

1.   Hook it to something—

It depends on your family's schedule, but it is good to connect family Bible reading with some other activity that happens daily. We are morning people, so we always had reading the Word of God connected with breakfast in our family. Everyone had to be at the table at a certain time, clothed and in their right mind, ready to hear the Word of God. If they wanted to eat breakfast, they had to have that already in front of them. This meant scheduling breakfast quite early so that they'd leave for school on time, which meant early bedtimes. This might not be the best plan for every family, but it works for us. To this day, Randy and I read the Word together every morning before going to work.

2.   Have something else to do at the same time—

Maybe this sounds like we took multi-tasking too far, but we found it helped our super-active kids to stay focused. When they were teeny-tiny, we would act out short little stories with them. I have happy memories of Randy putting the kids on his lap and acting out the story of the disciples on the storm-tossed sea. As preschoolers, the kids had Bible notebooks where they would "draw" the story that Dad was reading. This kept little hands busy and helped squirmy kids to listen. Later we gave them things to listen for, such as to listen to this chapter of Proverbs and tell the proverb that means the most to you. The family joke is that our youngest would always pick the first verse of any chapter as her favorite. Now that the kids are all grown, when we are together for a family Bible reading, it usually happens with everyone sitting around drinking gourmet coffee—the adult version of crayons as a concentration aid.

3.   Keep it short—

We found that we were better off reading a little together each day than a huge reading every once in a while. Someone told us that you should think of family devotions lasting as many minutes are your child's age. Ten minutes for a ten-year-old, etc. With a 9-year span in the ages of our children, the theory sort of broke down, but the principle of doing a little regularly is a sound one.

    4.   Keep it relevant—

Praying about daily concerns right after reading the Bible connected our daily reading to our daily lives.

Faithfully yours,

Deanna

WEEK 17—APRIL 23-29

Protected (vs. Vulnerable): Kept safe from danger or harm

"He who dwells in the shelter of the Most High will abide in the shadow of the Almighty. I will say to the LORD, 'My refuge and my fortress, my God, in whom I trust.'"
Psalm 91:1-2

Dear Moms at Prayer,

Yesterday in my devotional time, I read the story of the rape of Dinah. This morning I read an article in *Christianity Today* in response to the "#MeToo" movement. It reminded me that sexual abuse is a problem that has been around a LONG time. This week I have on my heart to pray for our children's sexual safety. We can pray against the evil influences of media, against abuse on whatever level, and for a godly, healthy perspective on sexuality. May the Lord protect and defend our children, no matter what their age.

Abiding in His shadow,

Deanna

WEEK 18—APRIL 30-MAY 6

Routine orderliness (vs. Random chaos): arranging my habits to reflect our commitments and priorities

"He went to Nazareth, where he had been brought up, and on the Sabbath day he went into the synagogue, as was his custom."
Luke 22:39a

Dear Moms at Prayer,

I am a routine person—I think it's the teacher in me. I function best when I do the same thing each Monday morning, and then move on to the Tuesday routine and then on through the week. That is probably the reason why I have been having a hard time getting this Moms at Prayer letter out on the right day. Home assignment just doesn't lend itself to routine.

Our kids need routine, also. Any kindergarten teacher knows the wisdom of regular schedules when working with little kids. At home, too, kids do well with some good habits enforced in their lives.

When our kids were still at home, we were not always the most disciplined people in the world, but we did have two steady patterns that we stuck with pretty much all the time. In the morning after breakfast, we always read the Bible and prayed together. It may have been a hurried affair if we were running late, but it was part of our regular routine.

The second habit was reading together in the evening. We just about always had a book we were reading through together. We read classics like *Little House on the Prairie* and *Little Women*. We read funny books (the *Mrs. Pollifax* series was a favorite when our kids were teenagers). And I don't even know how many biographies of international workers we read over the years. We jokingly blame our son's propensity to serving in dangerous countries to all those years of reading books like *God's Smuggler* and *Bruchko*. Having the kids beg for "just one more chapter" are some of my happiest memories.

Let's pray for the routines of our kids' lives. Pray that good habits will be formed, and godly, foundational disciplines will be built into their lives. Pray that, like Jesus, they will have "customs" that help them to grow into the men and women of God that they are called to be.

Routinely yours,

Deanna

WEEK 19—MAY 7-13

*Generosity (*vs. Stinginess): carefully managing my resources so I
can freely give to those in need*

*"Remember this: Whoever sows sparingly will also reap sparingly,
and whoever sows generously will also reap generously. Each of you
should give what you have decided in your heart to give, not
reluctantly or under compulsion, for God loves a cheerful giver."*
II Corinthians 9:6-8

Dear Moms at Prayer,

During our very first "tour" of speaking in churches, Randy
and I met Hazel and Edna Willey. It was the beginning of a long
relationship. Every time we went through Missouri, we stayed
with them. They were a working-class family. Hazel worked in a
factory and Edna sewed for people. In spite of their modest means,
they faithfully gave to our support each month. As our family
grew, they became Grandma and Grandpa Willey to our kids.

When our son was 14 years old, he was involved in a serious
accident. As I sat by my comatose first born in the intensive care
unit of a French hospital, Randy was busy communicating with
our worried family back in the States. During that time, Grandpa
and Grandma Willey called Randy. They had heard about David's

accident. They told us they had $5000 in the bank they were saving for retirement. They were ready to send it to us to help with David's medical bills.

Thankfully we were able to reassure them that we were covered by the French medical system and David's bills were all taken care of. We were never the same after that phone call. To think that this couple was ready to give their retirement fund to help our son was one of the most moving and humbling experiences of our lives.

Grandpa and Grandma Willey are in heaven now, but I will always be grateful for their legacy of generosity. I pray that my life and the lives of our children will honor their memory. May all our children learn the joy of managing their resources so that they can freely share with others.

Generously yours,

Deanna

WEEK 20—MAY 14-20

*Initiative (*vs. Idleness): recognizing and doing what needs to be
done before I am asked*

*"If anyone, then, knows the good they ought to do and doesn't do it,
it is sin for them."*
James 4:17

Dear Moms at Prayer,

I remember one Mother's Day when our kids woke up early
and fixed me a breakfast so Mom could have breakfast in bed. We
were in France at the time in an old, narrow house with a steep,
dark staircase. Our daughter was carrying the breakfast tray with a
plate of food, a glass of orange juice and a pot of coffee. You can
probably guess what happened. At some point on that treacherous
journey, the pot slipped, the tray tipped, and the beautiful
Mother's Day breakfast was history.

I tell this story to remind us that it is not always easy for kids
to learn the character trait of initiative. It is a risk to take the
initiative. It is easier to just hang back and go with the flow.

But any leader knows that there is a huge difference between
working with someone who is simply obedient and someone who
looks around, sees what needs to be done and does it. Great things

cannot be accomplished if there aren't people who are willing to take the initiative without being told what to do.

Even as a hostess, there is a huge difference between a guest who jumps in and makes him or herself useful and one that shows up at 12:30 to ask, "Is there anything I can do to help?"

That is why we need to encourage and teach our children to have the character trait of initiative. If they do, they will be appreciated by friends, admired by adults, put on the path to career advancement by bosses and ready to do great things for the Kingdom. Let that be our prayer focus for this week.

To get back to that famous Mother's Day morning, I heard the crash and went down to find my stairs dripping in coffee and my disappointed little girl in tears. The Lord gave me the grace to respond positively, even enthusiastically. I was so grateful for the effort and so willing to show how easily it could all be salvaged and so proud of her initiative, that I think she ended up satisfied with the whole effort.

Now, before you get too impressed with my parenting skills, I could also tell you about the time when our son took the initiative to take apart the expensive learning game his uncle gave him for Christmas because he wanted to try to figure out how it worked. I have to admit that when I saw that beautiful gift in a thousand pieces on the bedroom floor, I was not quite so encouraging or gracious in my response! It is a good thing that our children's characters are not dependent on our parenting skills!!

Proactively yours,

Deanna

WEEK 21—MAY 21-27

Wonder (vs. Jadedness): the ability to marvel at the unexpected
blessings of life

*"There are three things which are too wonderful for me, Four which
I do not understand: The way of an eagle in the sky, The way of a
serpent on a rock, The way of a ship in the middle of the sea, And
the way of a man with a maid..."*
Proverbs 30:18, 19

Dear Moms at Prayer,

Today I taught the ladies at the Nancy Pierce Institute (our
women's academy at the Faculté de Théologie Evangélique de
l'Alliance Chrétienne-FATEAC) how to make vases out of plastic
bottles. The finished efforts were quite nice. What touched me is
how excited the ladies got about this simple idea. They made
flower arrangements in their vases and left happy, triumphantly
carrying their new treasures.

As I watched them head home, I saw another character trait,
which, for lack of a better word, I'm calling "wonder." Wonder at
the little things. Astonishment seeing the unexpected blessings of
life. It is the opposite of blasé. It is that childlike perspective that
glimpses the miraculous in the everyday. It says, "Look Nana, see

the rainbow!" and "We got to build a fire and roast marshmallows and it was SO fun!" It is the ability to be enchanted by birds and snakes and ships and young love.

Wonder gives us joy in the little things. Last week my granddaughter excitedly told me how she had saved up to buy a sewing machine. "And Nana, it is SO amazing because you can even run it with a battery. That will be practical when we get electricity cuts, won't it?" Her tendency to wonder at the blessings was touching.

I want to pray that wonder take root in our children this week. I want to pray that they will have that child-like faith to see God's hand at work in their lives and in their world and to be filled with wonder. Our kids get to travel and see and do so much, that they can almost become jaded to the wonderful things happening around them. (Seriously? Another camel ride? Boring!) I want to pray that the Lord will protect them from cynicism and apathy. Instead, may He fill them with a godly enthusiasm and zest for life. I invite you to pray for wonder in their lives.

In awe of His glory,

Deanna

.

WEEK 22—MAY 28-JUNE 3

Farsightedness (vs. Shortsightedness): the ability to evaluate and process the events of our life with an eternal perspective

"Set your mind on the things above, not on the things that are on earth."
Colossians 3:2

Dear Moms at Prayer,

We recently lost the president of our seminary, a godly and widely appreciated African leader. It turned out to be a two-country, three-week, all-consuming process to honor and bury this wonderful man of God. During this same time frame, we've had the wife of one of our students pass away and one of our professors in the hospital.

Right now, sickness, mourning, death, and funeral preparations are a major part of every day. I don't want to be morose, but it has reminded me afresh of the brevity of our presence on earth. We live like we have forever in this world with our children, and later our grandchildren, but that is not the case. Our life on this planet is a vapor, a passing mist that comes and goes.

Of course, this life is not the end. If our children know the

Lord, we will have eternity together. Once, when we were saying yet another good-bye, I was bemoaning the fact that our family is spread all over the world and we can't get together very often. My son replied, "Yes, Mom, but we will have all eternity to hang out and catch up on everyone's news."

With these thoughts in mind, I propose that when we pray for our children this week that we pray for an eternal perspective. Let's ask the Lord to help us and our children to hold on lightly to this present life and to live with heaven in view. I'm all for practical prayers. However, when we pray for our children, let's not let the potty training and the struggles with phonics and the ups and downs of puberty and the soaring cost of college and the latest romance (or lack thereof) overshadow the timeless issues of character, salvation, and godliness.

Here's a great prayer from Ephesians 3:14-19 to get us started:

For this reason I kneel before the Father, from whom every family in heaven and on earth derives its name. I pray that out of his glorious riches he may strengthen you with power through his Spirit in your inner being so that Christ may dwell in your hearts through faith. And I pray that you, being rooted and established in love, may have power, together with all the Lord's people to grasp how wide and long and high and deep is the love of Christ, and to know this love that surpasses knowledge—that you may be filled to the measure of all the fullness of God.

Yours with an eternal perspective,

Deanna

WEEK 23—JUNE 4-10

Tenacity (vs. Irresolution): having the strength of mind to
strategically stick to God-given goals

*"Therefore, since we are surrounded by such a great cloud of
witnesses, let us throw off everything that hinders and the sin that so
easily entangles, and let us run with perseverance the race marked
out for us."*
Hebrews 12:1

Dear Moms at Prayer,

Last week we attended a seminar on the theme of "Finishing
Well." At first, I thought the subject was only applicable to us old
geezers. However, the more we talked about it and the more I
thought about it, the more I realized that everyone, at just about
any stage of life needs to know how to finish well. Our daughter,
Becky, only weeks away from graduating from college, is working
hard to finish well. Our son and daughter-in-law are struggling to
know how to finish one commitment and move on to another as
the security situation changes in their volatile region. And even
our daughter Cathy is praying that little Matthew will finish the
newborn baby stage and move into the "able to sleep for more than
a couple of hours without needing to nurse" stage.

Some of the keys to finishing well can be helpful at any transitional stage of our lives. Growing ever more intimate with God, maintaining a meaningful lifestyle, keeping connected to a supportive social network, and setting wise, significant goals may be great suggestions for retirement, but they are also smart moves for young folks in transition.

Let's pray for our children, that they will learn to finish each stage of their lives well and know how to transition into the next stage of their lives in a healthy and age-appropriate manner. Let's pray that they will have the perseverance to finish each stage of life well and the wisdom to know when it is time to move on to new commitments and projects. More than anything, let's pray that they be guided each step of the way in their life journeys with the Lord.

Tenaciously yours,

Deanna

WEEK 24—JUNE 11-17

Understanding (vs. Prejudgment): the discerning awareness that
leads to sympathetic and tolerant relationships

*"When one of the Pharisees invited Jesus to have dinner with him,
he went to the Pharisee's house and reclined at the table. A woman
in that town who lived a sinful life learned that Jesus was eating at
the Pharisee's house, so she came there with an alabaster jar of
perfume. As she stood behind him at his feet weeping, she began to
wet his feet with her tears. Then she wiped them with her hair,
kissed them and poured perfume on them. When the Pharisee who
had invited him saw this, he said to himself, 'If this man were a
prophet, he would know who is touching him and what kind of
woman she is—that she is a sinner.'"*
Luke 7:36-39

Dear Moms at Prayer,

Did you ever watch the TV series LOST? I found the
flashbacks used in that series fascinating. They would show a
person doing something, which would usually lead the viewers to
draw a conclusion, "Man, that person is terrible. I can't believe
he/she did that!" Then they would stick in the flashback, and you
would see what the person had been through. You still couldn't

condone the mistakes, but you at least understood where they were coming from.

Jesus was the master "understander." Without ever condoning sin, He understood where people were coming from and the motivations behind their deeds. We look at a person's actions, but God looks at their heart. He knew the woman washing his feet was a sinner, but he saw her heart of repentance and gratefulness.

I want my children to have hearts of understanding. I pray that they will have the discernment to see behind the behavior to the inclinations of the heart. I pray that they will have tender hearts to see the hurt and the needs of those who do things that are hard to understand. I want them to be willing to look at others who are hard to understand with eyes of love, able to see the potential and the possibility of each person as a creation of God. Please join me in this prayer this week.

Understandingly yours,

Deanna

WEEK 25—JUNE 18-24

Thoroughness (vs. Incompleteness): knowing what factors will diminish the effectiveness of my work or words if neglected*

"Whatever you do, work at it with all your heart, as working for the Lord, not for human masters, since you know that you will receive an inheritance from the Lord as a reward. It is the Lord Christ you are serving."
Colossians 3:23-24

Dear Moms at Prayer,

I am working on my doctorate and I am required to read a LOT of books. My method of reading has tended to be haphazard. I notice if I like the design on the cover. I read the back-fly leaf and make a snap judgment on the value of the book. Then I start at the beginning and just read. I always plan to underline and take notes and write a summary of each chapter as soon as I read it. However, half the time it doesn't work out that way. I end up reading in the easy chair by the fan in the living room and don't want to get up and find my highlighter. Or I have a glass of iced tea going on the side and don't want it to sweat on my notes. Or I get interested in what the author is saying and just read, thinking I'll remember it later. Or my pen doesn't work, and I end up sticking little torn bits of tissue paper in good sections, so I can come back and find them when I'm ready to take notes.

Then I hit the point where I have to write up a literature review and start desperately looking around for my notes, which are distributed in vaguely labeled document files, emails to myself and various random Word docs stuck on my desktop, not to mention scribbles on papers at the bottom of my purse, in my desk drawers and laying around on the top of my bedside table. I always get the work done, but I waste a lot of time because of my incompleteness during the process.

That is why I liked the definition of thoroughness written at the top of this letter. It is not a question of being so obsessive-compulsive that I think I must do everything. It is a matter of knowing what factors will diminish the effectiveness of my work or words if neglected. In other words, being smart in the way I work.

Thoroughness is such an important thing for our kids to learn. No matter what educational system our children are involved in, or what job they are trying to accomplish, they need to learn to work with thoroughness. This will establish their reputations as good students and workers and build godly character in their lives—not to mention saving them time and grief in the long run. I think this is one application of Colossians 3:23, *"Whatever you do, work at it with all your heart, as working for the Lord, not for men."* During this time of graduations, new jobs, transitions and goal-setting, this is a great prayer focus for our kids.

Thoroughly yours,

Deanna

WEEK 26—JUNE 25-JULY 1

Cautiousness (vs. Rashness): knowing the importance of right
timing in accomplishing right actions*

*"The wise are cautious and avoid danger; fools plunge ahead with
reckless confidence."*
Proverbs 14:16

Dear Moms at Prayer,

If anyone knows the importance of right timing, it is a mom
serving overseas. Let's think of a few examples:

It may begin with timing on when to start a family.

"Do I really want to be pregnant during language study?"

It continues through pregnancy and birth.

"How early should we drive down to the distant hospital for
the birth of the baby?"

Those early years...

"Is this a good time to hire a nanny?"

"Is Junior ready to go to a local pre-school?"

School years...

"Should I start homeschooling little Martha?"

"Should we take an early (or a late) home assignment to fit into
Suzy's school schedule?"

Junior high and high school...

    "Is Ralph ready for boarding school?"

    "Should we visit colleges during home assignment?"

    "Isn't Mary too young to have a boyfriend?"

And trust me, I can tell you from personal experience that the timing issues don't stop when the kids go off to college.

    Then, to make it even more complicated when praying for our children, somewhere along the line we have to transition from praying that we will know God's perfect timing and start praying that they will know God's perfect timing.

    Let's pray for the right timing in our children's lives each step of the way, that they will accomplish marvelous things for the Lord in HIS time.

Cautiously yours,

Deanna

WEEK 27—JULY 2-8

Humility (vs. Arrogance): acknowledging that achievement
results from the investment of others in my life*

"Humble yourselves before the Lord, and he will lift you up."
James 4:10

Dear Moms at Prayer,
   In international ministry circles, there are the Great Ones.
And then there are the rest of us.
   I remember speaking in churches in the States after a military
evacuation from Congo because of the war. People were impressed
by our sacrifice and dedication. It was kind of gratifying to be
admired and appreciated. But, invariably, conversations would
take a predictable turn. At some point someone would ask, "Do
you know Steve Woods[2]? Now, he has an impressive ministry."
Apparently, this Steve Woods had also come from the Congo, and
had marvelous things to share. We heard an unspoken, but clear
message. We were good, but Steve Woods was better.
   Ever had an experience like that?
   As parents, we sometimes find the whole issue of humility to
be a little challenging. We want our children to have strong,

---

[2] Not his real name.

healthy self-images, but we don't want them to be proud or arrogant. We want them to be humble, but not humiliated. James 4:6 says that "God opposes the proud but gives grace to the humble." We pray for that sweet humility in our children's lives that will enable them to receive the grace of God.

Humbly yours,

Deanna

WEEK 28—JULY 9-15

Virtue (vs. Dishonor): the moral excellence evident in my life as I
consistently do what is right*

"Who can find a virtuous woman? for her price is far above rubies."
Proverbs 31:10 (KJV)

Dear Moms at Prayer,

I read an interesting article the other day about virtue. It said
that although the word virtue is often presented in the feminine,
such as the virtuous woman in Proverbs 31, the Latin origin of the
word is masculine. (By the way, my daughter-in-law recently told
me that Proverbs 31 is her least favorite chapter in the Bible. It is
too guilt producing!)

My husband, the exegesis professor, is very critical of these
"look at the origin of the word and make up a new meaning"
processes, so take these thoughts with a grain of salt. Despite his
skepticism, I did look up the origins of the word virtue on
Wikipedia, which we all know as an extremely reliable resource,
right? Wikipedia concurs that virtue comes from Latin and had
connotations of manliness, honor, worthiness of deferential
respect and civic duty. It makes me think of a hero, who is brave
enough to choose to do the right thing, even in the face of
difficulties.

Dear Moms at Prayer

This week let's pray that our children would have the courage to choose virtue over vice, to be strong enough to do the honorable and respectful thing, no matter what the cost. May both our sons and our daughters walk in virtue, honor and righteousness.

Virtuously yours,

Deanna

WEEK 29—JULY 16-22

Justice (vs. Corruption): taking personal responsibility to uphold
what is pure, right, and true*

*"He hath shewed thee, O man, what is good; and what doth the
LORD require of thee, but to do justly, and to love mercy, and to
walk humbly with thy God?"*
Micah 6:8 (KJV)

Dear Moms at Prayer,

Growing up in Africa is an eye-opening experience. Poverty,
suffering, injustice—TCKs see these things even before they are
able to grasp the implications. I've seen two responses to this
situation in the attitudes of our children growing up
internationally. Some become calloused and ho-hum. They live in
their own little world and couldn't care less about anything going
on around them. However, that is the exception.

Most grow up with tender hearts for the suffering and a fire in
their bones for justice. They want to do their part to change the
world. One of the factors in developing that world-changing
perspective is intentional efforts to involve our kids in meeting the
needs of the oppressed and the needy.

It is thrilling to read about the wonderful outreaches and

ministries of our students in international schools. In Burkina, our youngest daughter's life was transformed by being involved in ministries to help orphans and the poor. I'm sure there are many other similar situations going on with our kids in other countries. These are life-transforming experiences that help our kids develop a godly perspective to their life in overseas and an awareness of the call of God on their lives.

As parents, we have a responsibility for cultivating in our children an interest in and a burden for the injustices that exist in our world. We don't need to wait until they get to a Christian high school or until some energetic youth group leader organizes something. We can pray and ask the Lord to show us how He would like our children to be involved in ministry right now. It will look different in different situations, and at the different stages of our children's lives. God wants to give our children a desire to make a positive difference in their world.

This may involve risk. I remember when our son got involved with a homeless shelter in France. When he was 15, he actually lived at a shelter in Paris for a week because he wanted to understand their world better. He loved it, but it felt a little scary to me at the time.

This will also call for Spirit-led creativity. I can't say what TCK ministry involvement will look like in Guinea or Russia or Taiwan. However, I am convinced that if we talk to the Lord about it, He will give us and our children age-appropriate, culturally acceptable ideas for getting involved.

Let's pray that God will give our children hearts for justice and show us our part in helping them grow in righteousness and truth.

Justly yours,

Deanna

WEEK 30—JULY 23-29

Sensitivity (vs. Callousness)*:* using my senses to perceive the true
attitudes and emotions of others*

*"Hannah was praying in her heart, and her lips were moving but
her voice was not heard. Eli thought she was drunk."*
I Samuel 1:13

Dear Moms at Prayer,

The story of Eli's reprimand of Hannah's prayer has always
been just a little annoying to me. Poor Hannah is pouring out her
heart to the Lord and Eli rebukes her for being drunk. Maybe
because of his own family issues, Eli totally misreads Hannah's
actions. A more sensitive person would have discerned Hannah's
desperation and her sincere crying out to the Lord.

Children can learn to have sensitive hearts. Even little ones can
be taught that a kid who brags all the time might just be covering
up insecurities. Even young people can learn to read between the
lines and discern the deeper needs of those around them. Children
can learn that even innocent teasing can hurt other kids' feelings.
They can learn to be aware of the hurt they may be causing. Our
children need to learn godly sensitivity to those around them.

Let's pray for sensitive hearts, both for our children and for ourselves. May the Lord help us not to jump to conclusions, but to help us to see beneath the exterior to the heart cry of those around us.

Sensitively yours,

Deanna

WEEK 31—JULY 30-AUGUST 5

Obedience (vs. Willfulness): quickly and cheerfully carrying out the direction of those who are responsible for me*

"Walk in obedience to all that the Lord your God has commanded you, so that you may live and prosper and prolong your days in the land that you will possess."
Deuteronomy 5:33

Dear Moms at Prayer,

Have you ever done the "little kid countdown"? You know how it goes:

Mom (who is in the middle of making bread and doesn't want to have to wash her hands and go out into the living room):

"Becky, please put that vase back on the shelf before you break it."

"Rebecca Lynn, I told you to put the vase back."

"Rebecca Lynn Harrison, put that vase back RIGHT NOW."

"Young lady, if you don't have that vase in its right place by the time I count to three, I'm coming over there and believe me, you don't want that to happen."

"One......, Two......., Two and a half........."

Am I the only one who has resorted to those kinds of threats?

I thought it was interesting that the definition of obedience involves the words "quickly" and "cheerfully." Ultimately, obedience is about attitude as much as it is about actions. No parent (including our heavenly Father) wants children to obey the letter of the law with a bad attitude, while they continue to circumvent the original intent and goal of the law. If they grow up with a willful and disobedient attitude, how will they learn to walk in obedience to the Lord?

This week let's pray for our children to learn a healthy brand of obedience that includes a cheerful attitude and a willing spirit.

Obediently Yours,

Deanna.

WEEK 32—AUGUST 6-12

Quiet (vs. Agitation): the ability to trust others and the Lord, and to avoid the agitation that comes from believing we need to fix everything

"Now about your love for one another we do not need to write to you, for you yourselves have been taught by God to love each other. And in fact, you do love all of God's family throughout Macedonia. Yet we urge you, brothers and sisters, to do so more and more, and to make it your ambition to lead a quiet life ..."
I Thessalonians 4:9-11a

Dear Moms at Prayer,

I am not exactly known for my quiet personality, to say the least. I think it is safe to say that I will never be a shrinking wallflower who silently sits by and lets life pass her by. However, in I Thessalonians, a quiet life is presented in the context of loving each other. Loving quietness is something I am working on and hopefully developing in my life.

What does this have to do with praying for our children? Well, for me, I am a fixer. If my children are in a pickle, I want to jump in and tell them how to get out of said pickle. My kids have a saying, "God loves you and MOM has a wonderful plan for your life." You may (or may not) be surprised to learn that my guiding words are not always enthusiastically encouraged by my children.

So how can I demonstrate a quiet, loving attitude toward my adult children and grandchildren?

1.   Trust in the power of prayer. I don't need to fix everything. I can pray and trust God to work in their lives.

2.   Be a good listener. I don't need to jump in and tell them about how the same thing happened to me and how I handled it. Maybe it's better to just be quiet and listen.

3.   Avoid certain topics. I have found I don't need to bring up the pros and cons of Calvinism to my decidedly Reformed-leaning son-in-law. Pacifism (especially with my Mennonite son-in-law), politics, child rearing philosophies and are-they-really-going-to-stop-with-just-two-kids-type discussions don't need to happen too frequently. The same goes for little kids. I can quietly ask them if they need to go to the bathroom, but I don't need to go on and on about how they had an accident yesterday.

4.   Be proactive with positive statements and exercise your ability to be quiet when it comes to criticism.

5.   If you do have something unpleasant to say, chose your time wisely. Little kids just hate it when you talk about the dumb (also sometimes unquestionably cute) things they did. I find with my grandchildren that they respond much better to my "corrections" when I take them aside and explain my concerns quietly.

This week I am praying about modeling a loving, quiet life in my relationships with my children and grandchildren, so that we can all walk in the quiet peace of HIS love.

Quietly yours,

Deanna

WEEK 33—AUGUST 13-19

Submission (vs. Rebellion): doing my duty with a good attitude

"Moreover, we have all had human fathers who disciplined us and we respected them for it. How much more should we submit to the Father of spirits and live! They disciplined us for a little while as they thought best; but God disciplines us for our good, in order that we may share in his holiness."
Hebrews 12: 9-10

Dear Moms at Prayer,

I'm going to tell you a true story that will probably shock you, especially if you don't believe in corporal punishment. Since our son is now in his 30s, I'm not worried about you turning me into social services. I am going to tell it like it happened.

When we were living in the Congo (then Zaire), there were very few places to go to get away. Sometimes we would drive out in the bush and spend the day with two older single colleagues to have a day off.

When our son was around 3 years old, we went out to visit the aunties for the day. In the afternoon, we were sitting around chatting and the kids were out playing. In the middle of our conversation, David burst into the living room brandishing a big, dirty stick, which he consequently threw on the floor. My husband told him to take the stick outside. He looked his dad right in the eye and said, "No."

Now, the stick was no big deal, but the defiance couldn't be tolerated. Randy gave David a swat and said, "David, you need to obey and take the stick outside." David took a deliberate stand and replied, "No." Another swat—just a little more convincing. Another request to take out the now significant stick. Another rebellious "No!"

By this time, the aunties were nervous, yours truly was embarrassed and the Stand-Off at OK Corral between father and son was in full swing. I'm not sure how long the request-spanking-defiance cycle lasted, but it seemed like an eternity. Finally, at some point, our little rebel without a cause was persuaded that his dad was not giving up and that maybe a stick in the house was not worth a sore bottom. He picked up the stick and carried it out of the house.

From that day forward, we saw a change in David. He may have done silly mistakes from time to time, but that attitude of defiant rebellion was broken. A submissive attitude is a priority when I pray for my children, and now when I pray for my grandchildren. How can our children obey God if they don't learn to walk in obedience in their family?

This week let's pray for the character trait of submission in our children. We don't all have to have the same beliefs on forms of discipline to join together for pray for this important subject. May our children learn to walk in submission with tender hearts their parents and to the Lord.

Submissively yours,

Deanna

WEEK 34—AUGUST 20-26

Gentleness (vs. Harshness): showing consideration and personal concern for others*

"Let your gentleness be evident to all. The Lord is near."
Philippians 4:5

Dear Moms at Prayer,

When we lived in France, we regularly had Jehovah's Witnesses come to the house. I remember a day when I had just finished reading a book which was the testimony of how a former Jehovah's Witness came to the Lord. In that book, I learned some things about JW doctrine. For that reason, when an unsuspecting JW team showed up at my door, I was ready to roll. I asked them about miracles (since I had learned in my reading of the book that they don't believe in miracles) and started into a machine gun-like recitation of all the healings and miracles I had seen in my life. I asked them to pray with me (since I had learned that they won't pray with non-JW's) and then fired out a wordy and self-righteous treatise on how sad it is that fellow seekers can't pray together. Every time they tried to get a word in edge-wise, I launched into another attack.

After they left, my then teenage son said to me, "Mom, why

were you so hard on them?" I started explaining how I was showing them the errors of their ways, but my words had a hollow ring. It gradually dawned on me that I had won the debate but had lost the chance to demonstrate the loving grace of Jesus.

I'm not saying we are required to spend hours listening mutely to JW half-truths. I am saying that our witnessing, our teaching, our ministries and our parenting should be cushioned in kindness and gentleness.

Now my son is called to serve among people of another faith. I have seen him in action with North Africans, East Africans and Middle Easterners. I am continually struck by the profound respect, graciousness and loving attitude that he demonstrates to those who don't share his beliefs. His example challenges me to biblical gentleness.

As I sit in Dakar, Senegal following the news of war-torn Cote d'Ivoire, gentleness seems forgotten in my context. However, I can choose to be considerate, to be polite, to be concerned about others and strive to be a peacemaker in a very non-peaceful world. I pray that the Lord will help me to be an example of gentleness to both my family and my neighbors as we pass this difficult time together.

Gently yours,

Deanna

WEEK 35—AUGUST 27-SEPTEMBER 2

Benevolence (vs. Selfishness): giving to others basic needs as an outflow of our love for God*

"He who is generous will be blessed, for he gives some of his food to the poor."
Proverbs 22:9

Dear Moms at Prayer,

Here in Cote d'Ivoire it is the season for paying school fees. Workers pull you aside to ask for loans. Official letters in flowery French (who do they get to write those letters, anyway?) explain why this year they need extra help. At prayer meetings, the subject of finances for kids' schooling comes up regularly. It's embarrassing for us and for them.

We and our children are the rich living among the poor. Let's pray for our children to have a tender, godly perspective towards the poor around them. May the Lord teach them to think of the needs of others. May they be preserved from an entitlement mentality and learn the joy of giving without receiving a reward.

Benevolently yours,

Deanna

WEEK 36—SEPTEMBER 3-9

Emotional health (vs. Emotional suffering): free from the
negative impact of physical and psychological trauma

> *"He has sent me to bind up the brokenhearted,*
> *to proclaim freedom for the captives*
> *and release from darkness for the prisoners..."*
> *Isaiah 61:1b*

Dear Moms at Prayer,

Last week was not an easy one. A dear Guinean brother, Moise
Mamy, was massacred by mob as he tried to minister to Ebola
victims. With the lightning speed of internet messages, we learned
about Moise's death before his son, Amos, who had arrived here
to study at FATEAC. We met with the seminary president, our
team leader and a student leader from Guinea to decide the best
way to break the news to Amos. During the discussion, our
seminary president said something that really hit me. He said that
we needed to make sure that Amos and Sylvie's little 10-month-
old daughter was not in the room when the terrible death was
announced. He did not want to have the baby absorb a bad
memory that would negatively affect her little spirit and bother
her later.

I thought about that statement and I wondered about our own children. Around the table they hear talks about Ebola and political instability and contingency plans. My own granddaughter, months after a friend was shot in the head by Al-Qaeda, said to her mom out of the blue, "Momma, remember when Uncle Jake was killed on my birthday?" Three-year-old girls should not have those kinds of statements in their vocabulary.

And yet, we know that if God has called us, He has called our children. We protect them as we can, but we can't protect them from everything. My prayer is that the Lord use the scary things our children see and hear not to harm them or traumatize them or scar them, but to create a heart after God's own heart that sees the world realistically and yet with compassion. Let's pray that the Lord will use even the hard times to work in our children's lives for good, to make them stronger and help them to walk closer to the Lord.

Trusting in His faithfulness,

Deanna

WEEK 37—SEPTEMBER 10-16

Persuasiveness (vs. Contentiousness): guiding vital truths around another's mental roadblocks*

"And he reasoned in the synagogue every sabbath and persuaded the Jews and the Greeks."
Acts 18:4

Dear Moms at Prayer,

When our son was little, he could talk anybody into anything. There was the time he told his younger sister that the tiny red-hot peppers that grow wild in the Congo were baby carrots to convince her to eat one. (That act did not, by the way, go unpunished!)

When he was in kindergarten, we were in the States on home assignment. Someone gave him a pair of Superman underwear with a matching tee-shirt. He put on the underwear over a pair of old tights he found, put rain boots on his feet and made a red apron into a cape. When he started to go outside in this getup, I tried to talk him out of it. I was sure the other kids would make fun of him. But he insisted. Within a few days the neighborhood was full of little boys running around in tights with apron-capes. That kid was persuasive!

Now he and his wife serve in the Middle East, and we can see why the Lord particularly gifted him in persuasiveness. In his situation, it is not just a matter of declaring a message. Careful study of the culture, an understanding of the historical background of the people, a wise use of vocabulary and a patient, persistent love and respect of the people in his life are vital for an effective communication of the Good News.

Not all our children will have the same calling. Nevertheless, all of them will need persuasiveness if they want to share their faith with those around them. It reminds me of the Apostle Paul who was willing to become all things to all men so that by all possible means some might be saved. This week let's pray for a Spirit-led persuasiveness for our children and for our own ministries.

Persuasively yours,

Deanna

WEEK 38—SEPTEMBER 17-23

Spiritual precocity (vs. Spiritual deferment): sensitivity to God's revelation early in life

"And Jesus grew in wisdom and stature, and in favor with God and man."
Luke 2:52

Dear Moms at Prayer,

Randy and I have been reading through Joel. Just to remind you of the circumstances, Israel is attacked by a locust invasion that is destroying the country. Joel reminds them that the Lord is *"gracious and compassionate, slow to anger and abounding in love."* Joel tells the people to call a sacred assembly and cry out to the Lord to save them.

Joel is a familiar story, but there was a phrase that jumped out at me when reading it this time. Joel 2:16 says,

Gather the people, consecrate the assembly; bring together the elders, gather the children, those nursing at the breast. Let the bridegroom leave his room and the bride her chamber.

God was calling the people to come to Him. He was not only calling the elders, He was calling the children, even the children who were still nursing. To me, this passage is powerful. Sometimes we have a tendency to disregard the spirituality of little children. However, here God is calling even the nursing babies to a solemn assembly to seek the favor of God.

This knowledge should change the way I pray for my 11-month-old grandson and my 2-year-old grandson and my 4-year-old granddaughter. This knowledge should influence the way we pray for our youngest TCKs. God is working in the hearts and lives of our children, even at a very young age. And our prayers can make a difference.

This week I am asking us all to pray for our younger TCKs. This could be our children or our grandchildren or other little ones that are a part of our lives. Let's pray that God will protect them, call them and help them to grow up in the nurture and admonition of the Lord, and that their hearts would turn to the Lord from an early age.

Grateful for the babies,

Deanna

WEEK 39—SEPTEMBER 24-30

Tenderness (vs. Roughness): responding with words and actions
that cause others to feel safe

*"Jerusalem, Jerusalem, you who kill the prophets and stone those
sent to you, how often I have longed to gather your children
together, as a hen gathers her chicks under her wings, and you were
not willing."*
Matthew 23:37

Dear Moms at Prayer,

This summer we went to East Africa to visit our adult kids.
While there I got a beautiful henna "tattoo" on my feet. Now,
several weeks later, I had just enough henna stain left to look like
I had been splashed with mud. I decided I needed a pedicure to get
a fresh look for the beginning of the FATEAC semester.

A local hairdresser has a little outdoor stand near my house
where she braids hair and does pedicures and manicures. Although
very rustic, the price is right, and it is a great place to hear local
gossip.

I've only been there a few times, and I've always had the same
middle-aged lady. She does a nice job. However, yesterday when I
went, a 20-something girl-in-training was holding down the fort.

She remembered me and was anxious to show that she could treat me just as well as the boss-lady.

Brushing off the fake hair extensions from her last customer, she settled me into a precariously broken plastic chair and set to work. What my pedicurist lacked in experience, she made up for in enthusiasm. My poor feet were washed, soaked, scrubbed, scraped, pumiced, exfoliated, massaged, rubbed and polished for an hour and a half (all for the equivalent of $6). I knew she was nervous, so I didn't want to criticize, but a couple of times I had to tell her she was hurting me.

At the end, my feet did look great with shiny rose-colored nails. However, when I got home, I realized that she had literally rubbed one of my heels raw and left an open sore. I ended up having to doctor my foot with antibiotic ointment and a Band-Aid. So much for a luxurious spa visit!

That whole experience got me to thinking about tenderness. Sometimes we can try to do the right thing, clean up the dirtiness of sin, scrape off the old dead skin of bad habits, either in ourselves or our children. However, if we don't administer our spiritual pedicures with tenderness, we might end up leaving wounds and scars.

I propose that this week we pray for our kids to grow in biblical tenderness, and for us to deal with others in a gentle spirit.

Tenderly yours,

Deanna

WEEK 40—OCTOBER 1-7

Punctuality (vs. Tardiness): showing esteem for others by doing
the right thing at the right time*

"Be devoted to one another in love. Honor one another above
yourselves."
Romans 12:10

Dear Moms at Prayer,

Right now, our daughter, Becky, is in her last week of the
semester before finals week. Because she has a double major in
cross-cultural studies and education, she has a lot of those time-
consuming projects that education teachers love to assign. They
are all due in the next few days. Punctuality will mean the
difference between good grades and bad grades. It's important that
our children learn about punctuality.

Sometimes among workers in Africa, I have seen a certain
justification for tardiness. "Oh, I'm just running on African time,"
they joke as they hop into a car full of people who have had to wait
for them for the last fifteen minutes. Obviously, African culture is
more people-oriented than task-oriented, and that can cause a
certain lackadaisical attitude towards consistent punctuality.
When you see all the responsibility our African pastors carry and

the constant stream of needy people in their lives, you can understand why they are often running late.

However, tardiness is not always evidence that we were selflessly giving ourselves for others. Sometimes it just signals a lack of discipline or a lack of esteem for those who might happen to be waiting on us. It often means that we have under-estimated the amount of time to accomplish a task before being ready for the next responsibility. We mess around and don't start getting ready "because we have plenty of time," and then we end up being late and making other people wait.

What does this have to do with our kids? Our consistent actions are the most influential teachers, as they model our heart attitudes to our children. Little eyes are watching how we spend our time and the choices we make. Let's pray that we will model respect and consideration with those in our lives.

Punctually yours,

Deanna

WEEK 41—OCTOBER 8-14

Responsibility (vs. Unreliability): taking ownership of my
thoughts, words, and actions

*"Now it is required that those who have been given a trust must
prove faithful."*
I Corinthians 4:2

Dear Moms at Prayer,

When I look back, we were rather hard on our kids. We moved from Congo to France when our son was 10 years old. Although he spoke Swahili fluently, he didn't speak a word of French. We just plunked him into the local French school, where he had to sink or swim. The teacher was saying, "Turn to page 41 and answer the questions," and David didn't even know how to say, "Where's the bathroom?" He cried a lot that first year. But he stuck with it.

When he was a teen-ager, he flew to Texas to spend his school break with Granny and Granddad. He got a job installing windows. This meant working in Texas heat (think Burkina in the hot season!) all summer. The next summer he got a job on a road construction crew. One of the worst parts of that job was biking to another city in crazy Parisian suburban traffic to work because he was too young to get a driver's license in France. Those jobs were long hours of hard physical labor. But he stuck with it.

Then there was the summer during his college years he got a grant as a research assistant of a big university math department. He quickly realized that he was way over his head and didn't have anywhere near the academic background of the other interns. He was publicly and privately humiliated and absolutely miserable the entire summer. But he stuck with it.

The funny thing is that we never once planned to make our kids suffer. It just worked out that way. And with every single one of those challenges in our son's life, I was sorely tempted to jump in and bail him out. But if Mom and Dad interfere and smooth out all the wrinkles of life, how will our kids learn to carry responsibility? Even Jesus learned by the things He suffered.

As I remember the years when our kids were at home, I know we didn't always get it right. Sometimes we did too much, sometimes we didn't do enough. But God was gracious through it all, despite our failings as parents. Today our son is a hard-working, responsible husband, father and international worker in a very difficult creative access country. To God be all the glory!

It is clear that we need to pray. We need to pray that we will be wise and discerning, knowing when to intervene and when to give our children the chance to overcome their difficulties without our help. We need to pray that our children will mature and learn responsibility through their challenges and their hard times.

Let's pray that our children will learn responsibility. Let's pray that rather than making excuses, they will learn to keep their promises. Let's pray that they will learn to work hard and do things to the best of their ability. Let's pray that they will know and do their duty.

Responsibly yours,

Deanna

WEEK 42—OCTOBER 15-21

Certitude (vs. Anxiety): structuring my life around that which
cannot be destroyed or taken away

*"The name of the Lord is a strong tower: the righteous run into it
and are safe."*
Proverbs 18:10

Dear Moms at Prayer,

Our middle child, ever the activist, is very concerned with immigrant families being separated in the States. She recently posted on Facebook, and I asked her permission to share her post with you. I think it shows the need for our kids to feel secure and safe, even in a very unsecure and unsafe world. It reminded me that what might not be a big deal can be a big deal for a little one. From a FB post:

> *When I was 5 or 6 years old in a crowded Congolese market, a vendor thought it would be interesting to see what my hair felt like. As my mom walked on to the next vendor, assuming I was by her side, this woman held me back, stroked my hair and laughed when I screamed for my mom. In the craziness of the market, it took my mom at the most 10 minutes to realize I was*

not with her and to come back and get me. This is pretty much the only time in my childhood I remember a Congolese person not being extremely kind to me. But it was one of the scariest moments of my childhood, watching my mom walk away and being held back from her by a stranger. It was scarier to me than when civil war broke out and we evacuated to the sound of gunfire in the distance. It was scarier than my first day in public school in a language I did not know when I was 8 years old. If I felt this much fear in 10 minutes, I can't imagine what the children at our US border are experiencing. It grieves me that we are inflicting this kind of trauma on children and their parents.

I think after she wrote this, it must have occurred to her that this might worry me, so she put in the comments:

This comment is for you Deanna Harrison: having navigated loud, crowded markets with kids, baskets of groceries and a long shopping list, I totally understand how this could so easily happen. Please do not feel guilty about this. In all reality it could have been just 2 or 3 minutes and felt like 10 for me. Love you!

Let's pray for our children to have a growing realization of the security that we have as we walk with the Lord.

Securely yours,

Deanna

WEEK 43—OCTOBER 22-28

Confidence (vs. Fearfulness): believing in the reliability, wisdom and love of God for my life

"Some trust in chariots and some in horses, but we trust in the name of the LORD our God."
Psalm 20:7

Dear Moms at Prayer,

I remember a time when our son, David, was around 3 years old. We traveled way out in the bush to visit some colleagues and help at a Bible School. David immediately made friends and was soon playing with a crowd of admiring Congolese children.

Around dusk, we realized that we didn't know where David was. We looked all around the old style "station," up to the Bible School housing, over to the pastor's house, down to the clinic. David was nowhere to be found. The pastor started organizing everyone to systematically look for the lost white kid. Someone ran over to the Catholic convent and asked around, but no one had seen anything. They even sent a group to go down to the river to see if they could find a floating body. (THAT was NOT encouraging!) After an hour of mobilizing local believers in a manhunt and quite a bit of extremely scary conjectures on where he could have ended up, lo and behold, some one noticed his little curled up body on the veranda of the house. He had crawled under a piece of rattan porch furniture and gone fast asleep. Thus ends one of those scary moments you live to laugh about later—but you hope that you only go through once!

This morning I saw a post on Facebook that reminded me of that incident. Another overseas mom had posted that three of her boys had gone out exploring and had not returned. Assurances of prayer were flying fast and furiously when we got a post saying that the boys had been found and were safe and sound. I think I know something about how she felt.

All this prompts me to suggest that this week we pray for our children's safety. For the little precious ones on the way, we can pray against miscarriages and lung masses. For younger ones, it may be getting lost or getting sick. For older ones, it may be car crashes or bullying or struggling with their faith at college. Wherever our children are, they need the protection of the Lord.

Thankful for His faithful watch over my children,

Deanna

WEEK 44—OCTOBER 29-NOVEMBER 4

Freedom (vs. Bondage): the ability to choose and act
independent of maleficent influences

*"It is for freedom that Christ has set us free. Stand firm, then, and
do not let yourselves be burdened again by a yoke of slavery."*
Galatians 5:1

Dear Moms at Prayer,

Our daughter, Becky, has arrived safe and sound in Cote
d'Ivoire to do a semester of student teaching at the International
School. You are hearing from one happy mom today!

Usually we don't think much about American holidays here in
Africa, but now that Becky is student teaching at the International
School, we are more aware of the seasons. The International
School seems to be into all things American. The irony in this is
that Becky's class has students from Norway, Spain, Italy,
Lebanon, many different African countries—and exactly zero
students from the States! In any case, today is Halloween and
everyone dresses up and parties. All of the sudden, for the first
time in a long time, I am aware that, in some parts of the world,
this week is all about goblins and ghosts.

While Becky is getting ready for her Halloween party, I am

going over my notes from my women's class. While discussing Galatians 5:1, our theme verse for the year, I was amazed at the subjects that came up with this group of African ladies: Female Genital Mutilation, generational curses, blood sacrifices, initiation ceremonies and growing up in polygamous families, among other things. When these ladies talk about finding freedom in Christ, they are not just whistling Dixie. There are scary, hurtful, traumatic forces out there, and when believers find freedom in Christ, it has the power to literally transform their lives.

Obviously, our children aren't fighting the same battles as the African students. However, the forces of darkness are real, although their strategies are different in different cultures. It struck me again with the tremendous need to pray for our children and the tremendous power there is in prayer. Whatever their situation, they need to find and walk in the freedom that only Christ can give.

On this October 31st, let's pray for children that they will find freedom in Christ, and learn to walk in that freedom daily.

Yours for freedom,

Deanna

WEEK 45—NOVEMBER 5-11

Assurance (vs. Alarm): awareness that God and others are
watching over me

*"Are not two sparrows sold for a farthing? and one of them shall not
fall on the ground without your Father. But the very hairs of your
head are all numbered. Fear ye not therefore, ye are of more value
than many sparrows."*
Matthew 10:29-31

Dear Moms at Prayer,

Randy and I just finished a visit in Brazzaville. The explosion
in Brazzaville was the day after we left. To my surprise, I received
this email from my daughter-in-law in the Middle East:

> We heard from a friend tonight, requesting prayer for people
> there in Brazzaville with a daughter named Hannah, who
> was very scared by the explosions (I can imagine!). I
> wondered if these are your colleagues? We are praying for
> them and for all the people who have been affected by this
> terrible tragedy. I just hate even thinking about it.

Isn't that wild? Here I am sitting in Boma, Democratic Republic
of Congo and get an email from my daughter-in-law in the Middle
East who is praying for a little girl named Hannah who lives in

Brazzaville where I just did a Regional Educational Consultant visit.

This gave me two thoughts for this week's prayer. The first thought is that we don't even know who all is praying for us. There are people who heard from someone who heard from someone that they should pray for us, and now they are lifting up our names to the throne of grace. That's a mind-boggling and comforting thought for me.

The second thought is that we need to pray for our kids as they experience trauma and insecurities. I know there were troubles in Bobo this week, and Senegal is unstable, and refugees are pouring into Burkina from Mali. Our kids hear the explosions and listen to the rumors and sometimes absorb the insecurities more than we realize.

Let's pray this week that our children would grow up with a sense of security that can only come from the Lord, the rock that can never be shaken.

Aware of His protecting presence,

Deanna

WEEK 46—NOVEMBER 12-18

Trustfulness (vs. Doubt): believing in the reliability of the Lord
in the circumstances of our lives

"And my God will supply every need of yours according to his riches
in glory in Christ Jesus."
Philippians 4:19

Dear Moms at Prayer,

Randy and I are still in East Africa, enjoying our son, daughter-in-law and grandbaby as we wait for the green light to go back into Cote d'Ivoire. We recently had the privilege of meeting Brandt and Pam Prince, who serve in the Congo. They came across Lake Tanganyika for the Christmas holiday.

Pam and her family live in the Shaba region of Congo. Roads, electricity, internet and running water are unreliable or non-existent. Available groceries are mostly limited to rice, manioc, papayas, bananas and a few locally grown greens. To make it worse, her husband has a medical condition and can't eat beef. The chickens are scrawny, and the fish are boney. Feeding her husband and three growing boys can be a challenge.

Pam is a beautiful Southern Belle from Arkansas. I was cutting her hair one day, and she shared a wonderful testimony with me. I knew that this testimony would be perfect for our Moms at Prayer letter. When I asked her if I could share her story, she was reluctant and embarrassed. However, with a little encouragement, she wrote out her story and gave me permission to share it. I wish you could hear her tell this in her charming southern drawl the way she shared it with me the other day. May it be an encouragement to all of us of the love of our Father and the power of prayer.

Testimony from Pam Prince:

I'm willing to give this testimony because I believe it gives glory to God even though it puts me in a really bad light so here goes:

I live in the Democratic Republic of Congo and life there is a little hard. It's very difficult to even get food to eat. The local people eat ugali and some sort of green leaves every day and occasionally add some dagaa (small, fresh-water fish) to it. I don't like to eat like that and one day I was really kinda fussing to the Lord, telling Him how life was so hard, and we just couldn't get any good food there and how I didn't like struggling to just put food on the table, etc., etc. I felt like the Lord spoke to me and said, 'I can get you anything.' I'm sorry to say I was in a mood, and the thought came into my mind, 'okay then, how about shrimp and strawberries' Those are two of my most favorite foods and I know for sure without a doubt they are NOT in my part of the world. Anyhow, I came out of my mood and actually forgot about it. A few days later, a Congolese man I know came to my house and he asked to see me. When I saw him, he pulled out a bag of frozen shrimp from Europe and asked if I eat shrimp. I literally nearly fainted on the spot and I said, 'Where did you get that?' He said, 'A UN worker got it and didn't want it and so he gave it to me and I'd like to give it to you.' Congolese people in our area are extremely poor and would never ever just give you something like that. I said, 'You mean you want to sell it to me?' He said, 'NO, I feel like I should give this to you.' I thanked him and went inside and began to cry my heart out to the Lord, asking for His forgiveness for my attitude and also my unbelief. A couple of days later, a neighbor (Congolese) called me and asked me to come to her house. When I got there, she said someone from Europe had brought her fresh strawberries and she knew I loved them and so she wanted to give them to me. Again, the tears came. The Lord began to supernaturally provide food for us. It would be a very long testimony indeed if I told you all the times in the last 6 months that God has put food on our table but I will say, that I have learned a big lesson, God can do anything, anywhere, any way He wants to do it and He wants us to trust Him for everything and not put limits on Him. I am learning.

In honor of Pam's testimony, this week let's pray especially for the physical needs of our children. This could be praying for food or medical care or school supplies for our younger children. It could go all the way up to jobs and financial supply for our adult children. Along with this, let's pray that each provision will build trust in our children, that they will learn to lean on the provision and the faithfulness of God.

Trustingly yours,

Deanna

WEEK 47—NOVEMBER 19-25

Gratefulness (vs. Ingratitude): letting others know by my words and actions how they have benefited my life*

"We give thanks to God always for all of you, constantly mentioning you in our prayers."
I Thessalonians 1:2 (ESV)

Dear Moms at Prayer,

There is a strange phenomenon at work in my life. Every week I find myself particularly challenged in the character trait that is coming up. This week was no exception. The subject was gratefulness and I had a lot to be grateful for. After all, we were safe in Dakar, Senegal while others were dodging bullets. We were staying in a beautiful borrowed home while colleagues were in tents in the Abidjan French military camp. My husband and I were together whereas several of our friends had one spouse trapped in Cote d'Ivoire while the other waited and prayed in Europe or the States. We had plenty to eat while our FATEAC students were unable to get out and buy food.

But instead of counting my blessings, I concentrated for two or three days on whining, pouting and explaining to anyone who would listen about how incredibly hard it was to be a refugee. I'm grateful for understanding leaders and incredible counselors who patiently and without condemnation helped me to work through what I like to call my "Eeyore Tendencies."

It is so easy to slip into a mode where we expect special treatment because we are international workers, instead of being grateful for those who voluntarily and sacrificially give to make our ministries possible. Even more dangerous is the possibility of inadvertently communicating ungratefulness to our children by our conversations and remarks. Let us pray against this in our own attitudes and the attitudes of our children.

If gratefulness is honoring a person who has invested in your life, then obviously our greatest debt of gratitude should be to our wonderful Lord who invested His very life for our salvation. But my prayer is that the Lord will open my eyes to recognize the many other people who have invested in my life and the lives of my children, that I may live a lifestyle of gratefulness.

Gratefully yours,

Deanna

WEEK 48—NOVEMBER 26-DECEMBER 2

Thankfulness (vs. Cynicism): recognizing and appreciating the grace of God working in every part of our lives

"Give thanks in all circumstances, for this is God's will for you in Christ Jesus."
I Thessalonians 5:18

Dear Moms at Prayer,

Celebrating Thanksgiving always reminds me of my most embarrassing holiday moment. At the time we lived right by a garbage dump and had a terrible rodent problem. We had put out poison but hadn't seen any results.

For Thanksgiving Day, we invited several expatriate families over to celebrate with us. After a great potluck dinner, the ladies were in the kitchen putting away food and getting desserts ready to serve. In the middle of pie-slicing and coffee perking, a very sick rat crawled slowly to the middle of the kitchen, keeled over and breathed his last. Can anyone spell awkward?

My guests were all good sports, took it in stride and told their own rat stories while I disposed of the corpse. Then a funny thing happened. The next year, someone else volunteered to host Thanksgiving dinner. I wonder why?

I feel somewhat vulnerable telling that story, but with the passage of time, I remember the fun of celebrating with friends more than the humiliation of what is now referred as "The Rat Incident". Remembering that fiasco has comforted me as I seek a godly perspective for this Thanksgiving and for this year with Moms at Prayer.

When I look back at prayer requests for this last year, I see situations much more devastating than my silly little "light affliction". The first things that hit me are the challenges and the disappointments. Just naturally speaking, the tragedies stand out to me more than the victories. I want to wrap my arms around every grieving mom who lost a child or grandchild, every struggling mom who is forced to stand by and watch her child suffer, and every desperate mom who is crying out to God for the salvation of her children. Where are all the happy-ever-afters? Does Romans 8:28 legitimately apply today?

Yet how can I fail to acknowledge the continual grace of God in our journeys? Together, we have experienced so many answers to prayer, so many loving miracles in the lives of our children, so many surprising twists and turns that could only be the hand of God. And overarching every circumstance there is the eternal perspective that our loving God is still on the throne.

Thankfully yours,

Deanna

WEEK 49—DECEMBER 3-9

Awareness (vs. Self-centeredness): the ability to be mindful the needs of others

"Is not this the kind of fasting I have chosen: to loose the chains of injustice and untie the cords of the yoke, to set the oppressed free and break every yoke? Is it not to share your food with the hungry and to provide the poor wanderer with shelter—when you see the naked, to clothe them, and not to turn away from your own flesh and blood?"
Isaiah 58:6-7

Dear Moms at Prayer,

Our granddaughter, Esther, had a favorite doll appropriately named "Dolly." Bought by her Granny (my mom) in a thrift store, Dolly had been loved on, cuddled and dragged around the Middle East, America, and West, South and East Africa. Dolly had special outfits (made by yours truly) designed to fit different occasions. She had an *abaya* and a *hijab*, a *boubou* and a Guinean indigo dress.

When Esther and her family moved to East Africa, she made a friend with a little African neighbor named Fatma. Whenever Fatma came to play, she went straight for Dolly. Esther, Fatma and Dolly spent many hours playing house together.

Not too long ago, Esther's family had visitors from the States, and they brought her some spiffy new toys. I'm not sure what went on in Esther's little 5-year-old mind, but the next time Fatma came to play, Esther gave her Dolly. Esther told her mom that she had so many more toys than Fatma, and Fatma loved Dolly so much, that she thought it was the right thing to do.

Our daughter-in-law got a bewildered phone call from Fatma's mom wanting to make sure that Dolly actually was a gift and that Fatma hadn't done anything wrong to take her. She was profuse in her thanks and told about how happy Fatma was to have her very own baby doll.

Later Esther had a case of "giver's regret", but she stuck with her commitment. She sometimes goes over to Fatma's house to visit Dolly, but she knows that she can't take Dolly home with her now.

I tell this story, not only to brag on my granddaughter (which I am totally doing!), but also to talk about a character trait that I'm calling "awareness." I see this akin to, but slightly different from, generosity. It is that tender heart, that listening ear, that open eye that sees the injustice in the world and longs to take just a tiny step toward addressing that injustice that we see so much in the message of the prophets.

This week let's pray that our kids develop the character trait of awareness. We can pray that they won't be calloused and blasé about the suffering around them, but that we also listen to the voice of a compassionate God to ease that suffering, even in small, child-like ways.

Proverbs 14:31 "Whoever oppresses a poor man insults his Maker, but he who is generous to the needy honors him."

Attentively yours,

Deanna

WEEK 50—DECEMBER 10-16

Dependability (vs. Inconsistency): fulfilling what I consented to
do, even if it means unexpected sacrifice*

*"One who is faithful in a very little is also faithful in much, and one
who is dishonest in a very little is also dishonest in much."*
Luke 16:10

Dear Moms at Prayer,

I guess most of you know that we have been in "voluntary
house arrest" mode the last few weeks because of the unstable
political situation here in Cote d'Ivoire. To make life even more
complicated, the government closed the airport and all the
borders. Way back in October I had committed to coordinate the
translation for the Church Planting Movement Conference
which will be held in Senegal next week. On Sunday I was sitting
in my snug, safe apartment wondering about the possibility of
leaving for Dakar in two days. Even if I could get out of the
country, I wasn't particularly thrilled with the prospect of leaving
my husband back in Abidjan. What if the borders closed again and
I got stuck in Senegal by myself? Not the way I had planned to
spend the holiday season. Our college age daughter, with her own
memories of being evacuated from Abidjan in high school, was
worried and concerned about the possibility of Mom and Dad

getting stuck in different countries.

On Sunday evening I was mulling all this over. I'm embarrassed to admit that I actually started thinking it would be nice if the borders just stayed closed. Then I wouldn't have to go to this stupid conference, stress myself with translation and get separated from my husband. Randy and I put out a sort of fleece that we would find out that the borders were open by Sunday if I was supposed to go to Senegal. Sunday, we went to bed at 9 pm and promptly fell into a carefree sleep. However, at 9:30 pm a friend called and told me they were opening the borders. I was still half asleep and trying to digest this news when the Lord spoke very clearly to me. "You know that the character trait for this week is dependability. Were you really going to write about it but not live it?"

Oops—sorry about that, Lord.

But wait, the plot thickens. Yesterday our team met and decided that we would all go to Senegal for the next couple of weeks to give things a chance to settle down in Cote d'Ivoire. Consequently, I'm not leaving my husband after all. He's coming with me.

I'm still sad to leave Cote d'Ivoire not knowing what the future will hold. However, I pray that the Lord will help me to grow in my faithfulness to Him and teach me to be an example of dependability.

Let's pray that our children will learn to be dependable, willing to fulfill their commitments even when they must sacrifice to do it. And join me in praying that the Lord will make us models of dependability that our children can look up to.

Dependably yours,

Deanna

WEEK 51—DECEMBER 17-23

Contentment (vs. Covetousness): realizing that God has provided everything I need for my present happiness*

"But godliness with contentment is great gain."
I Timothy 6:6

Dear Moms at Prayer,

Until recently, I hadn't put much thought into the fact that this year will be our first empty nest Christmas. However, a few days of holing up in our lonely apartment (to avoid possible civil unrest due to the upcoming elections) and a few hours of cruising the net trying to figure out what to send to our far away kids for Christmas left me in a melancholy mood. It was too easy to think of my sister. She loves the Lord. She is a good Christian. She will be surrounded by her children, her son-in-law, her future daughter-in-law and her grandbabies this Christmas. AND she'll have our daughter visiting her for three weeks.

As I was thinking my "poor me" thoughts, I'm not kidding when I say that an almost audible voice spoke to my heart. "Embrace it." At that point, I knew I had a choice. I could feel sorry for myself and compare myself to others or I could choose contentment. I have so much to be grateful for, so much to celebrate. I am separated from my children because I have the privilege of serving the Master in Africa and because my kids are doing amazing things with their lives. Would I seriously want to change that?

It is so easy for both parents and children to compare themselves to others. It might not be the same comparisons for the parents (Her house is nicer. His French is better.) as it is for the kids (He's faster. She's prettier). We all struggle to live contentedly with who we are and what we have.

I can't talk about children and contentment without mentioning the temptation to compare our kids. (Her son is smarter than mine. His daughter is more mature than mine.) Sometimes our urgent prayers for the improvement of our children are little more than outpourings of our own covetousness.

Let's pray for godly contentment, both for us and our children. May our heart attitude reflect I Timothy 6:6: *"But godliness with contentment is great gain."*

Contentedly yours,

Deanna

WEEK 52—DECEMBER 24-31

Resourcefulness (vs. Wastefulness): making wise use of what
others might overlook or discard*

*"He also that is slothful in his work is brother to him that is a great
waster."*
Proverbs 18:9 (KJV)

Dear Moms at Prayer,

For TCKs and international workers, Christmas can be the
best of times and the worst of times. On the one hand, we want
Christmas to be special. We want to give unique gifts. We want to
create traditions and draw the family closer together with
meaningful celebrations.

On the other hand, Christmas can be downright challenging.
Where do you get nice gifts for your family without spending an
arm and a leg? How do you avoid the "if it's not from the States
it's no good" syndrome? When the only reasonably priced
shopping mall is the *yugu-yugu* open-air used clothes market, what
are our options?

Resourcefulness is one area where most TCKs (and their
moms) can shine. I have seen families come up with impressive
options using locally available materials, not just for Christmas,

but for all kinds of occasions. Cool costumes for plays, neat birthday presents for friends, awesome toys made with local materials—African challenges help our kids be more creative.

Somehow, the very fact that there is a challenge makes the results more precious. Although it's a little wobbly, I will always treasure the wooden nativity set that my son made me one Christmas. Gifts our daughters sewed or embroidered or crocheted were always my favorite.

One of the key differences in international families that I've noticed is between those who mourn all they left behind and those who get excited about discovering great things where they are. Let's pray for resourcefulness for us and for our children. Pray that they will have the eyes to see the beautiful things the Lord has made available to them and the creativity to figure out how to use those things.

Resourcefully yours,

Deanna

ABOUT THE AUTHOR

Deanna Harrison is a mother of 3 children and grandmother to 6 grandchildren. She has a Doctorate in Intercultural Studies from Fuller Theological Seminary and has served for more than 40 years in cross-cultural ministry in the Democratic Republic of the Congo, France, Burkina Faso and Cote d'Ivoire. She currently teaches Practical Theology at FATEAC--the West Africa Alliance Seminary. As the coordinator for Moms at Prayer, she has been instrumental in promoting, encouraging and inspiring prayer for the children of global servants in Africa since 2010.

For more information about the author see Entrust Publications, www.entrustpublications.com.

Made in USA - North Chelmsford, MA
1318729_9780988762855
06.15.2022 1536